the ART of PUNS

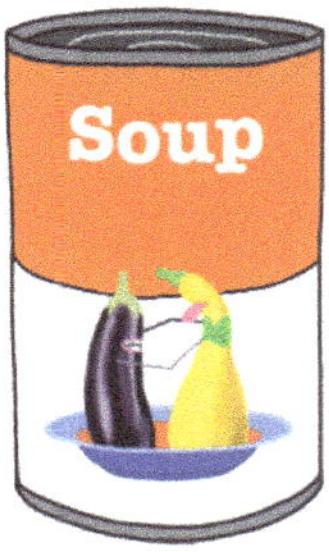

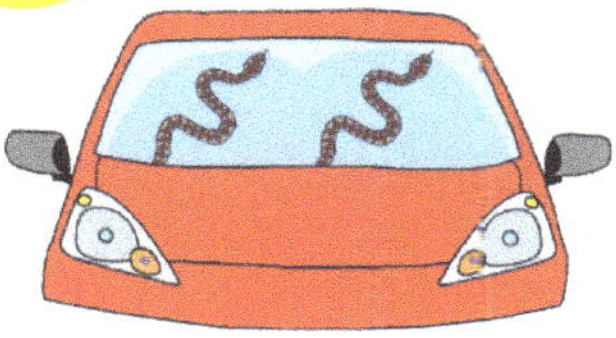

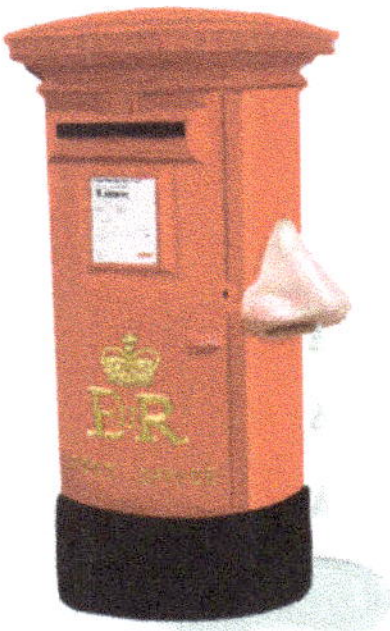

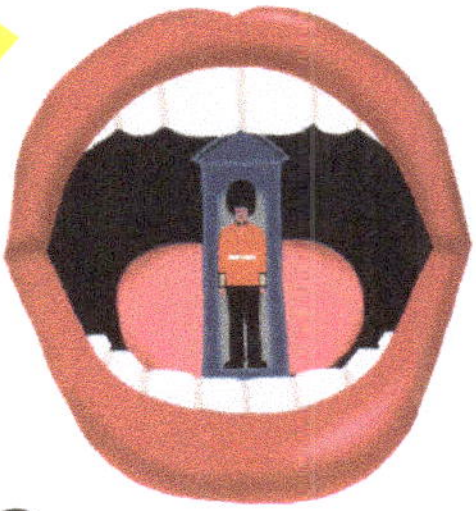

Illustrated Word Play

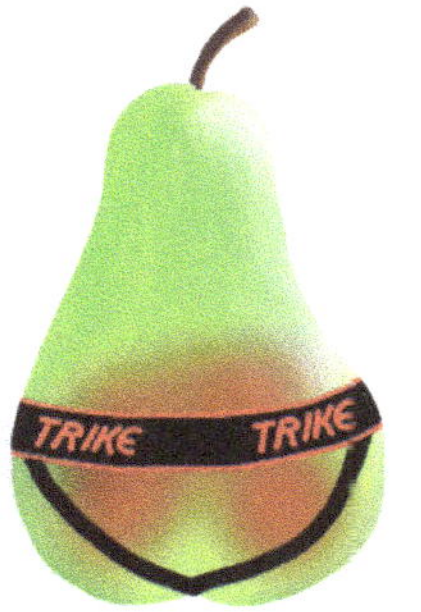

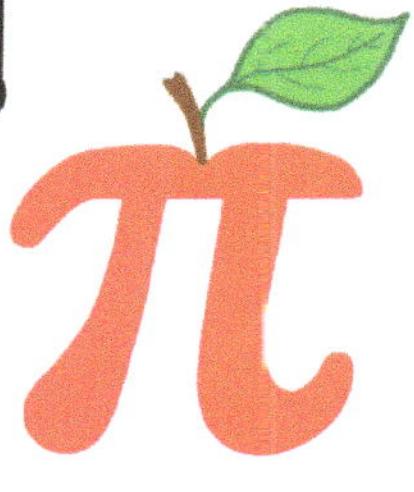

by George Wachob

ISBN: 0-692-84057-5
ISBN-13: 978-0-692-84507-3

Forward

"The Art of Puns" is a full color book of 100 illustrated and groan-worthy puns. Drawings of everyday objects, flora, fauna and anatomy are combined in unexpected ways to create the pun artwork. Titles on each page reveal the intended word play, and the humor is both unique and refreshing. Some puns are more challenging than others, but readers will have a hard time not smiling page after page.

Although teenage or adult viewers are more likely to understand the intended humor of the puns, children pre-school age and up are drawn to the bright colors and humorous art this book provides.

Pun Art Imprinted Items

Many of the graphics in this book are also available as designs on a variety of products produced by Zazzle. These items may be viewed and purchased by visiting:

www.zazzle.com/TheArtofPuns

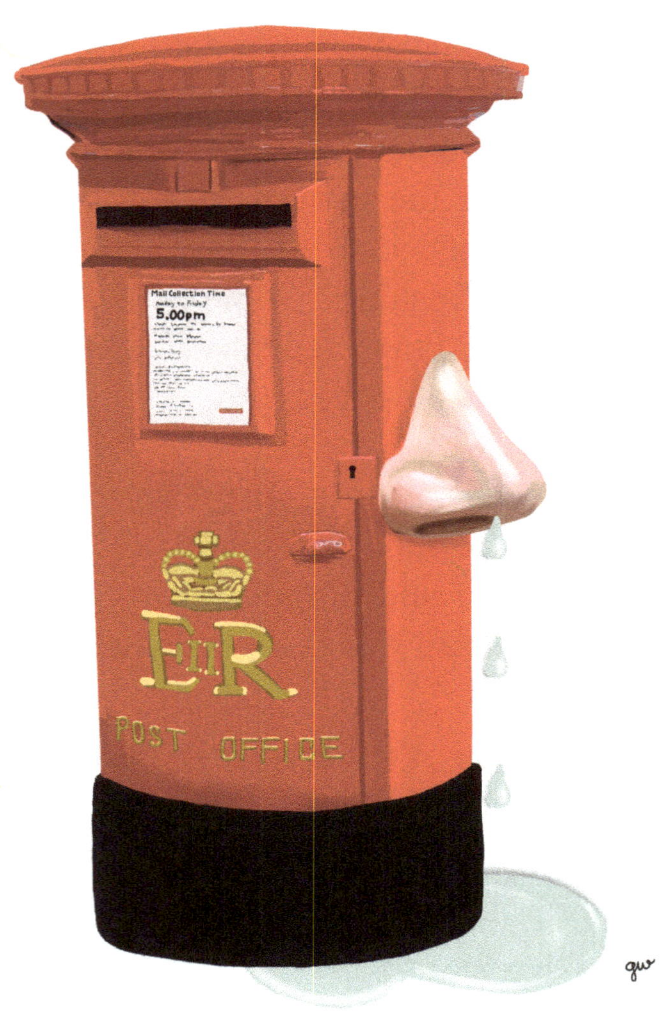

Post Nasal Drip

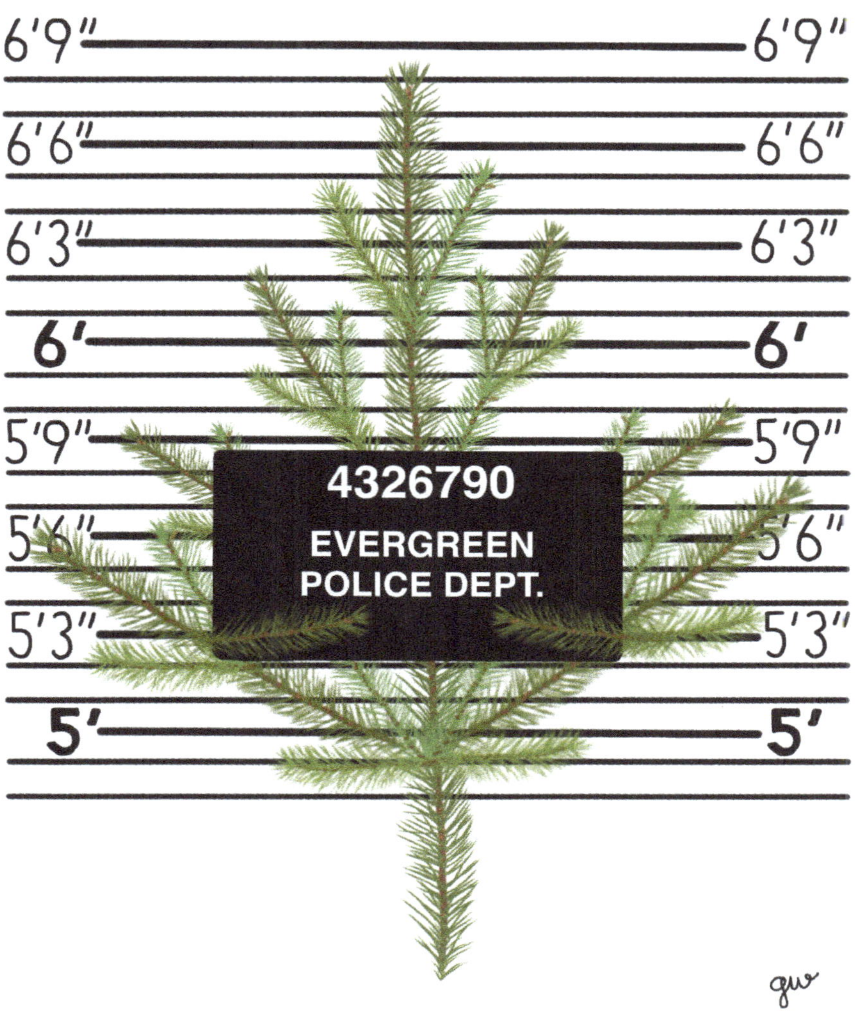

Naughty Pine

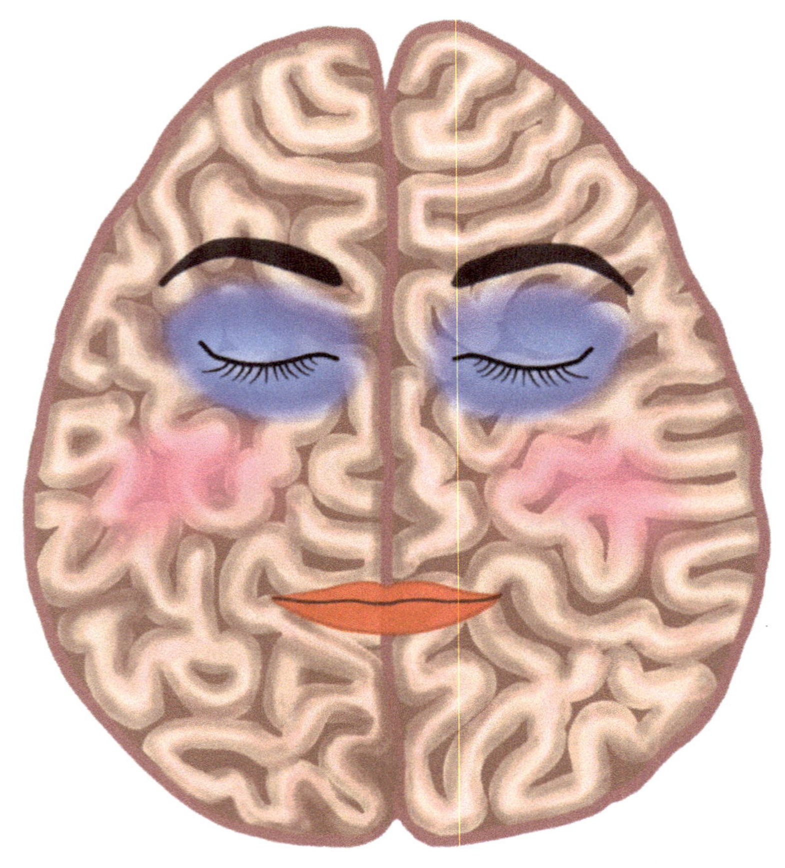

Makeup Your Mind

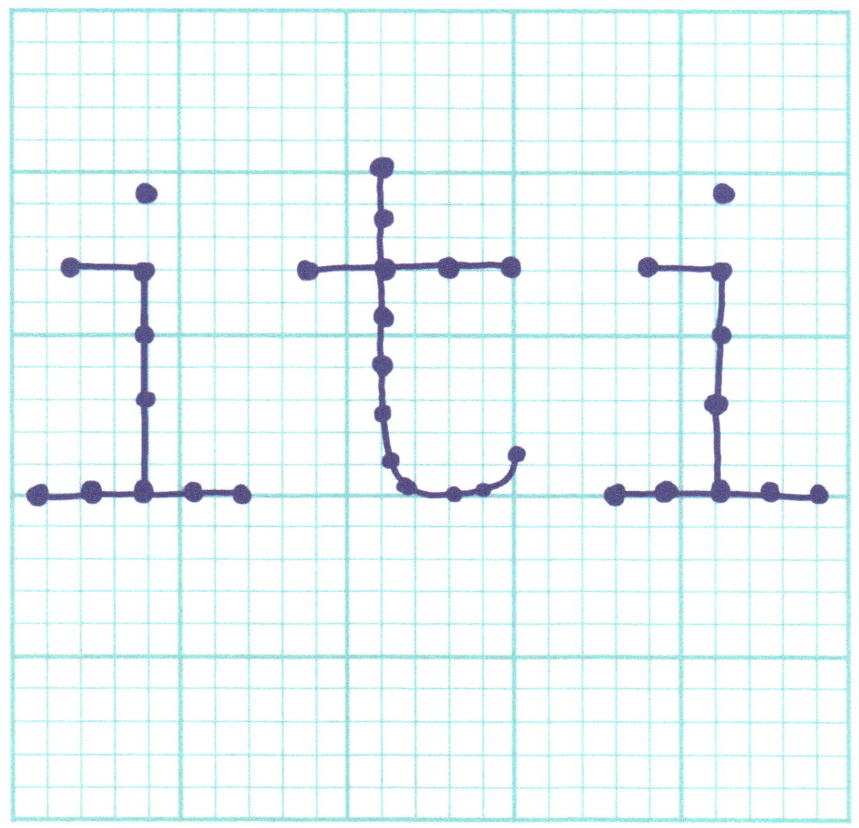

Graph "iti"

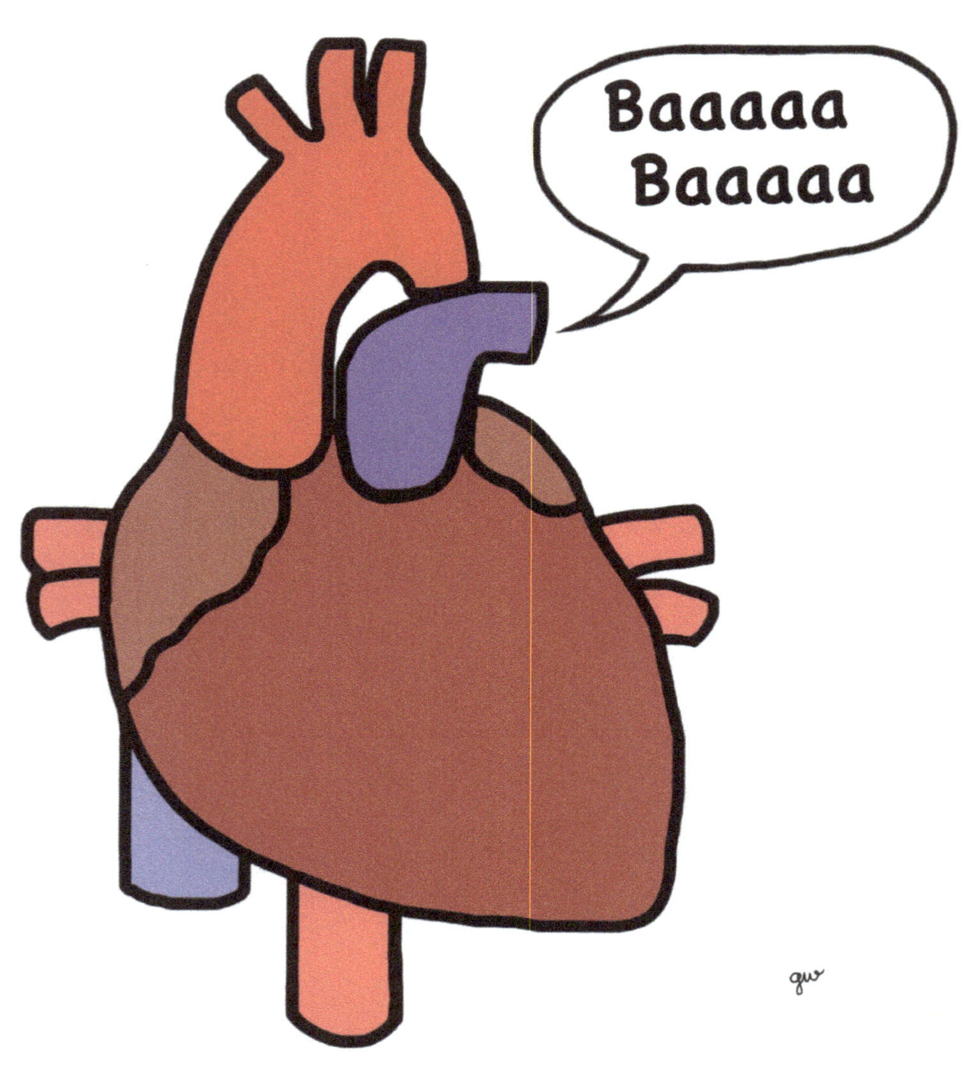

Bleating Heart

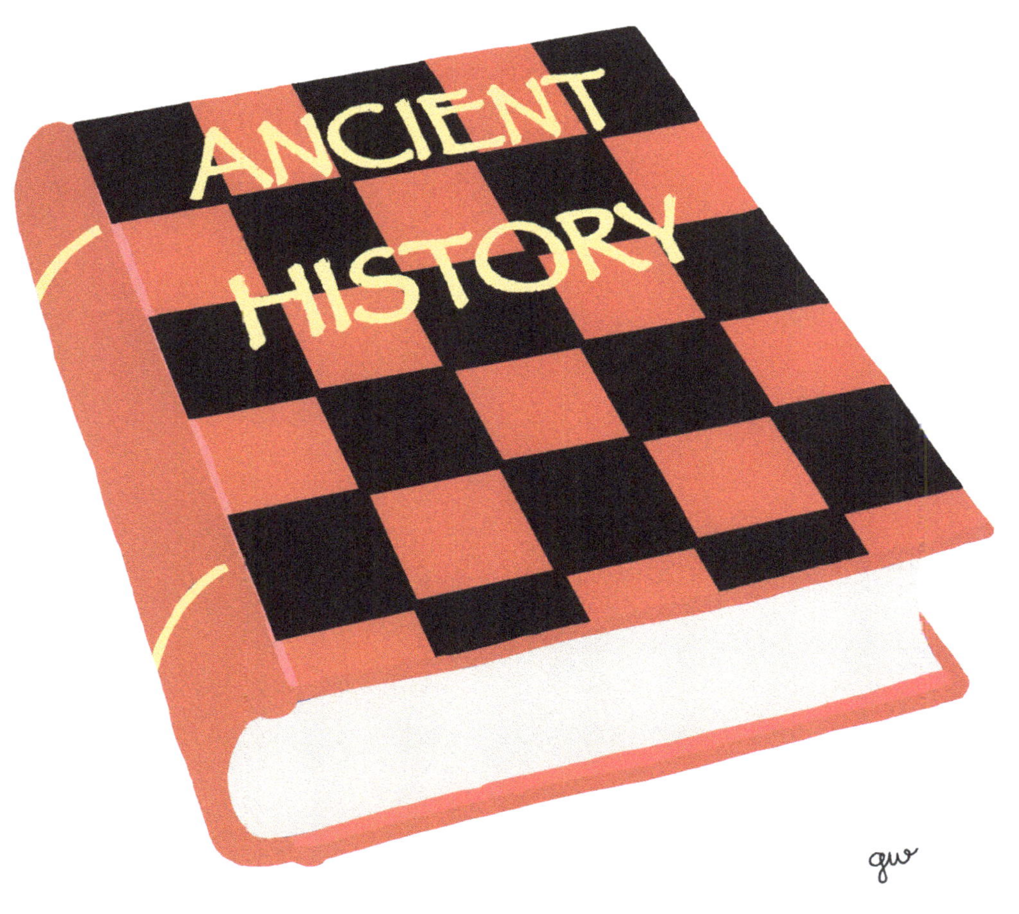

Checkered Past

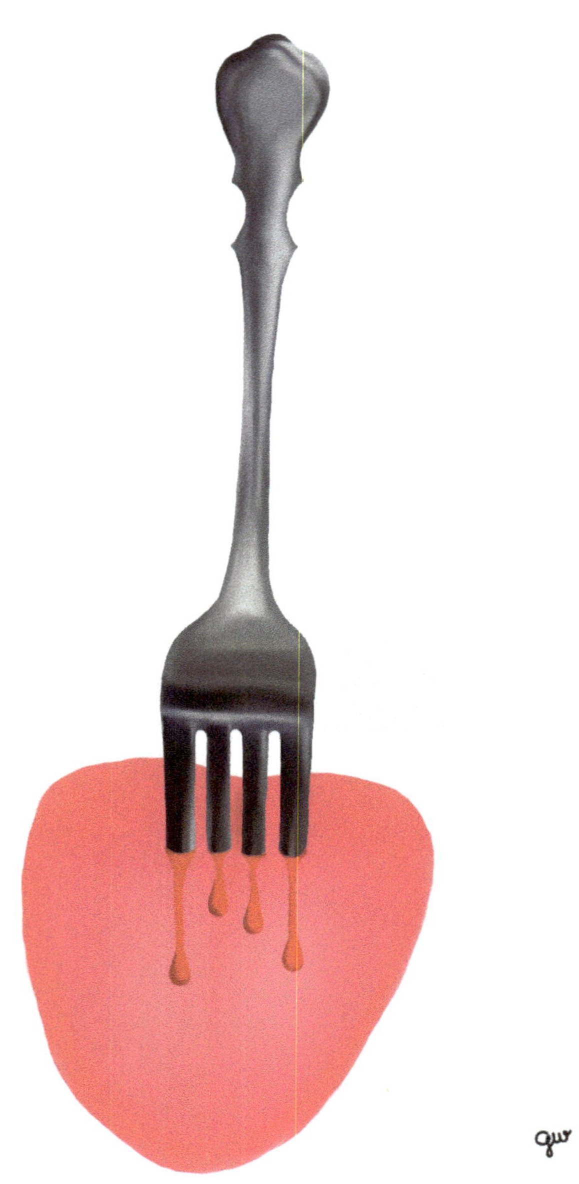

Forked Tongue

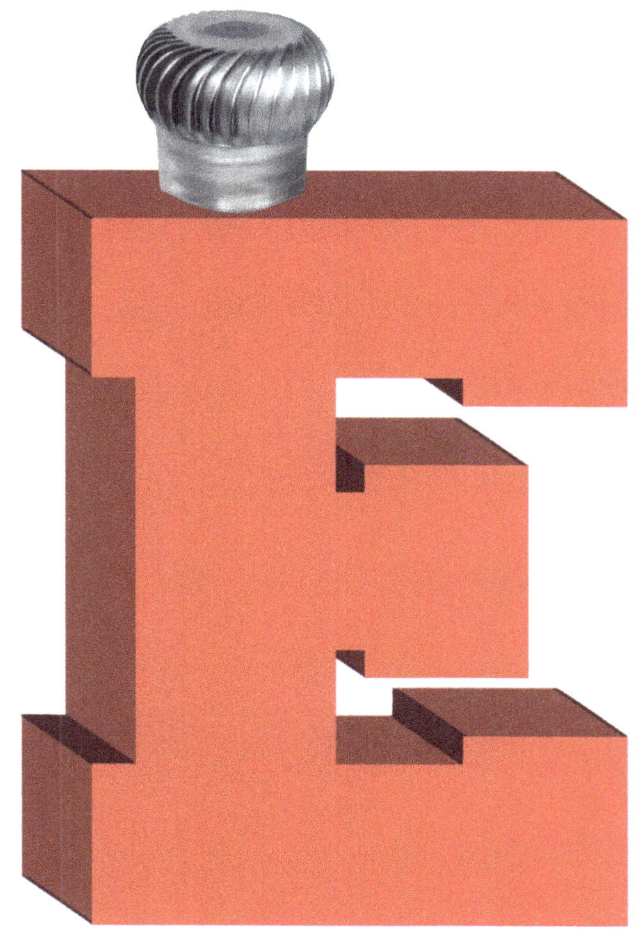

gw

E Vent

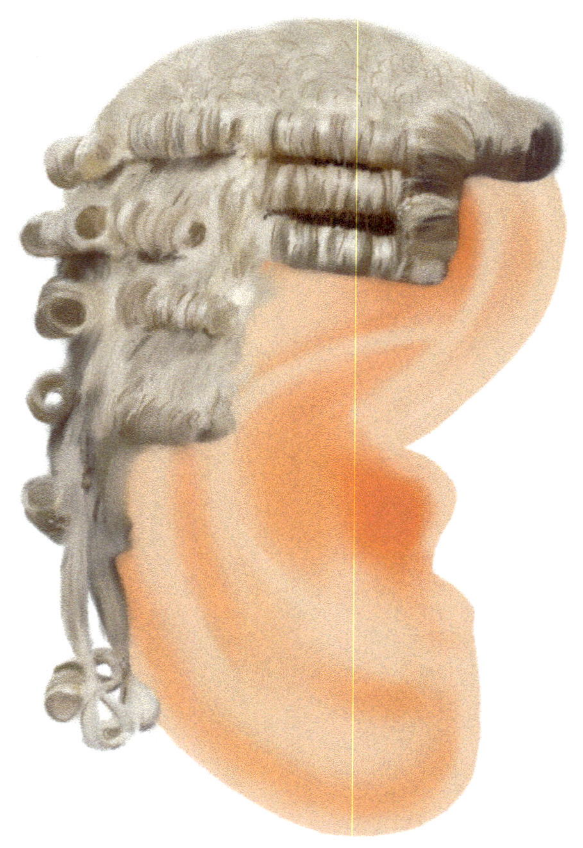

gw

Ear Wig

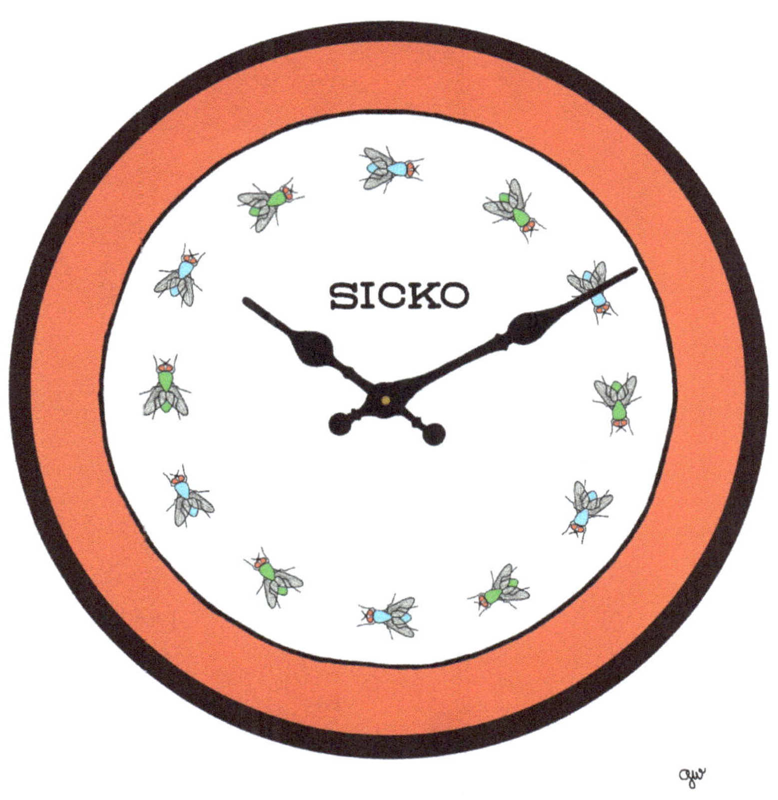

Time Flies

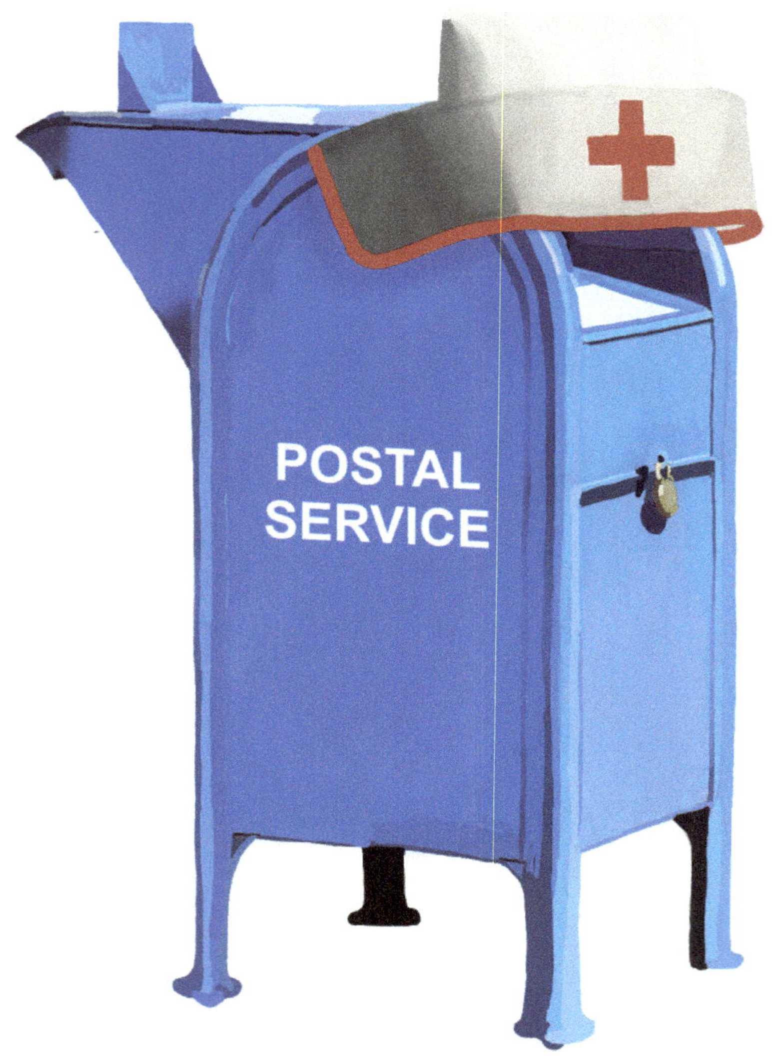

Mail Nurse

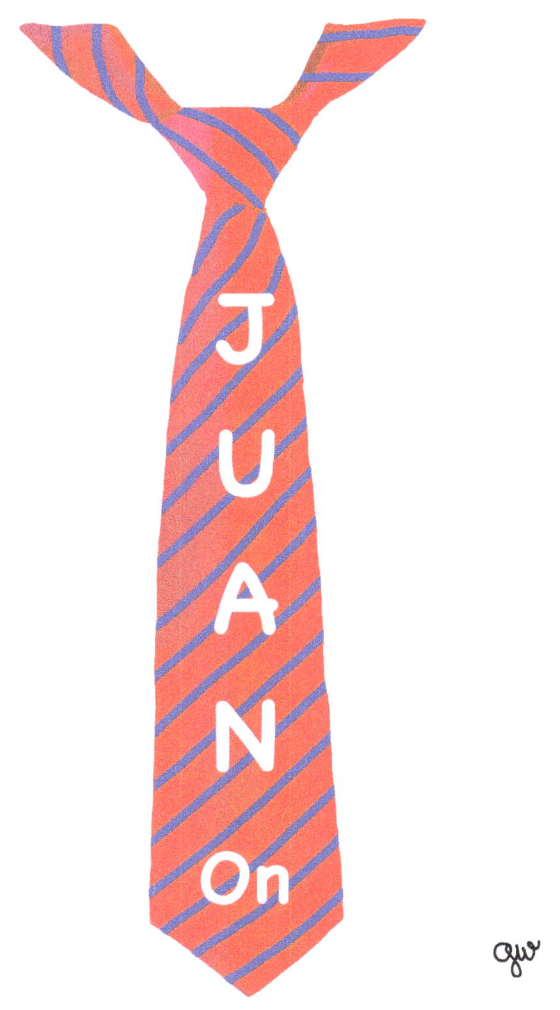

Tie Juan On

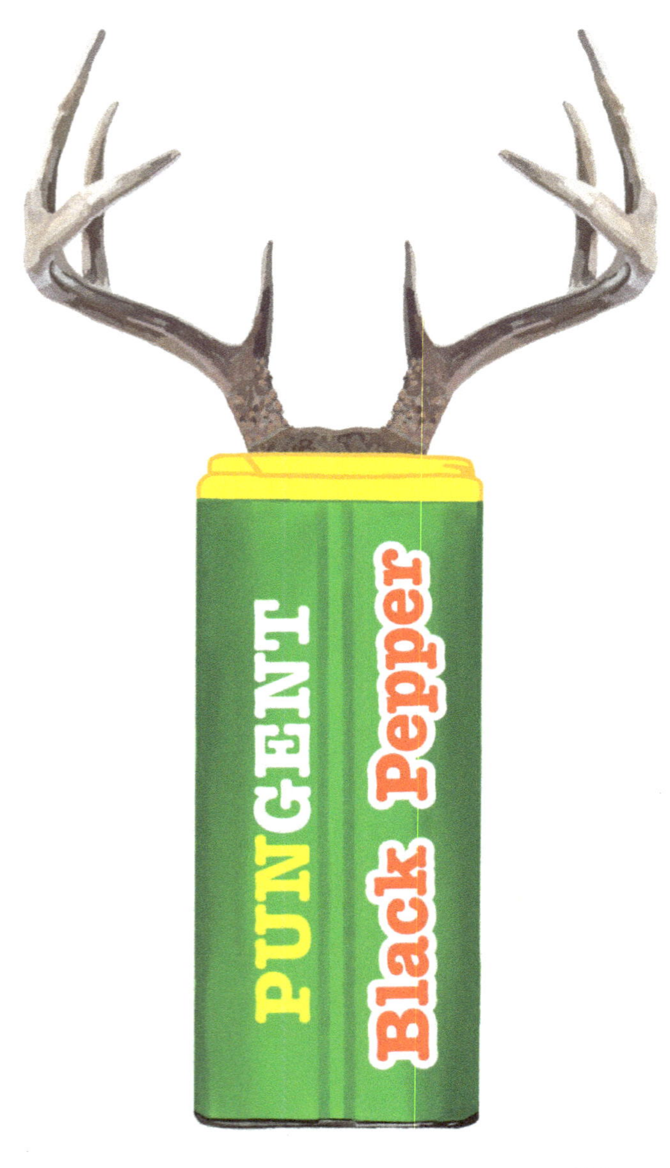

Spice Rack

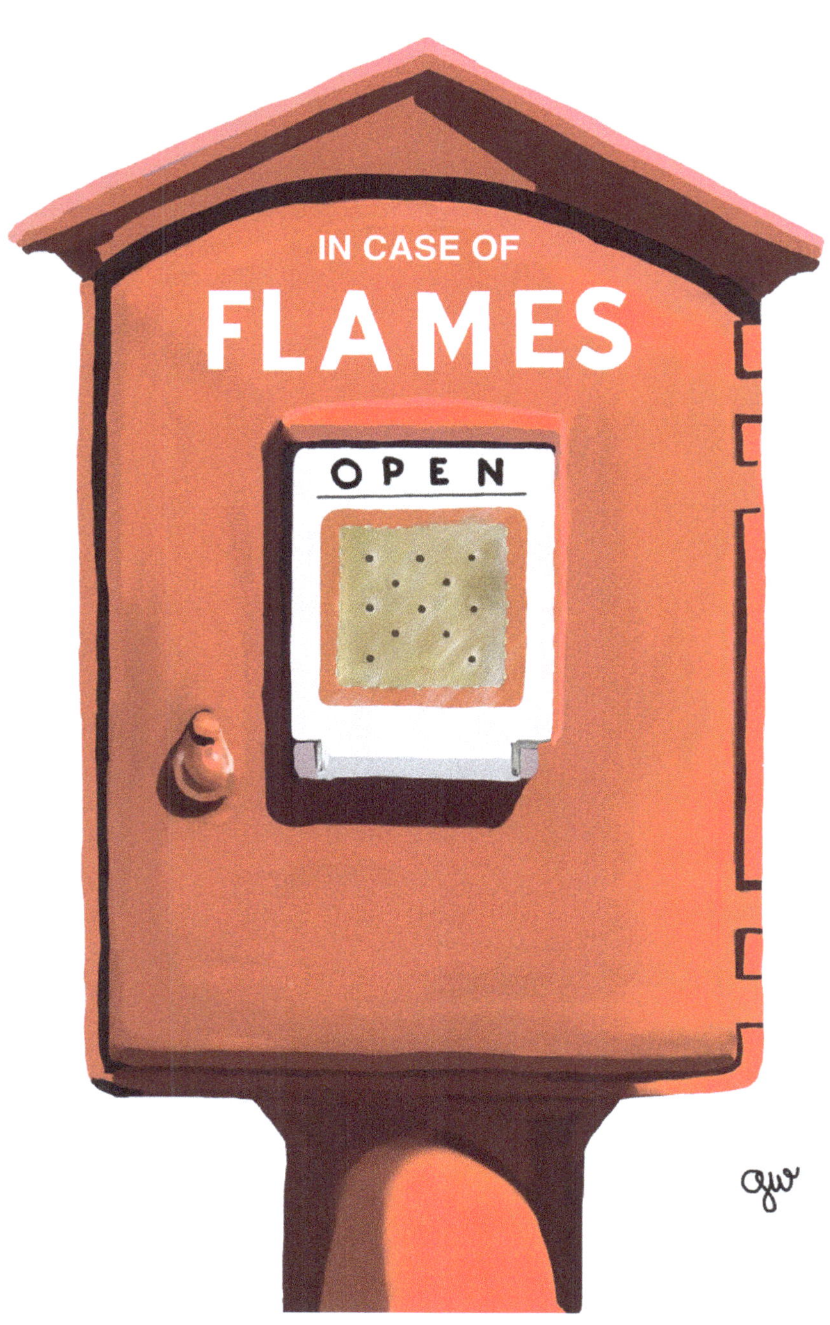

Fire Cracker

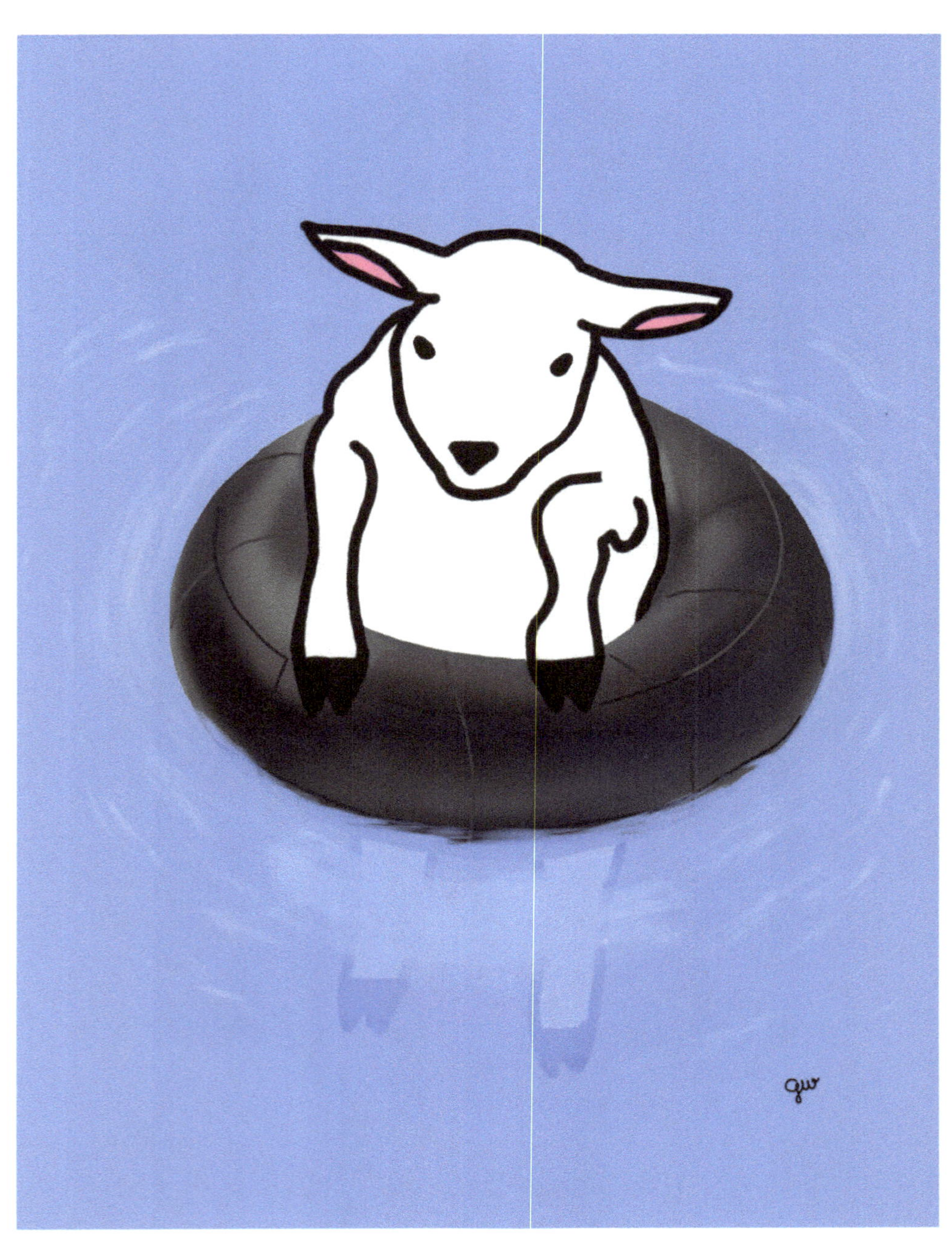

Ewe Tube

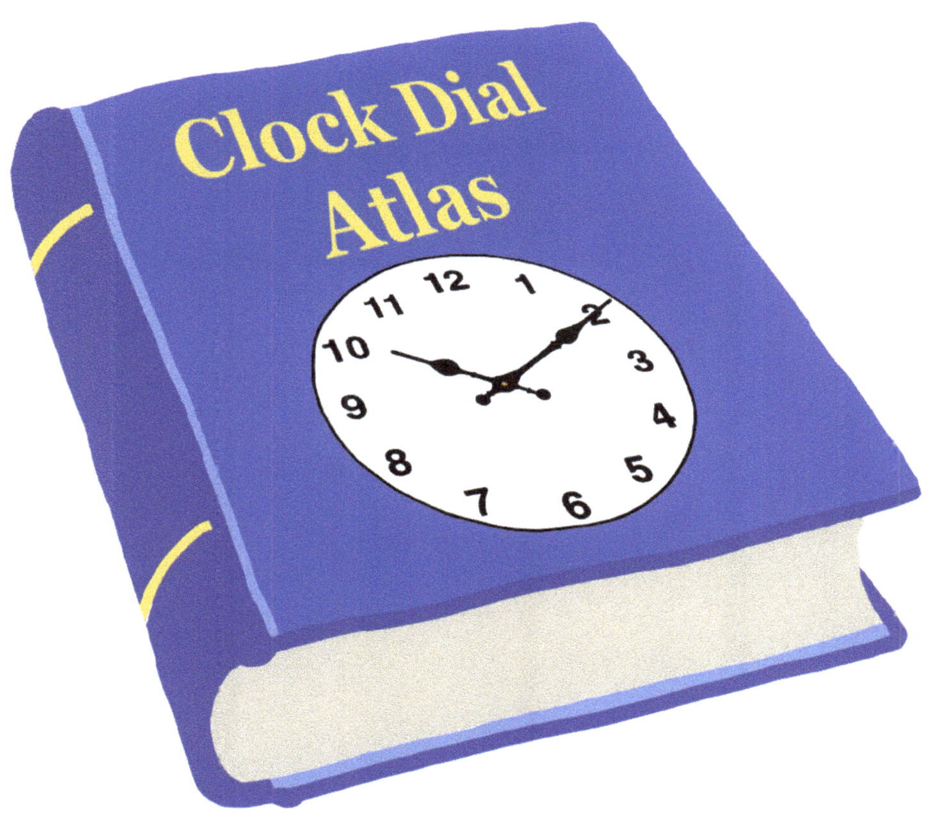

gw

Face Book

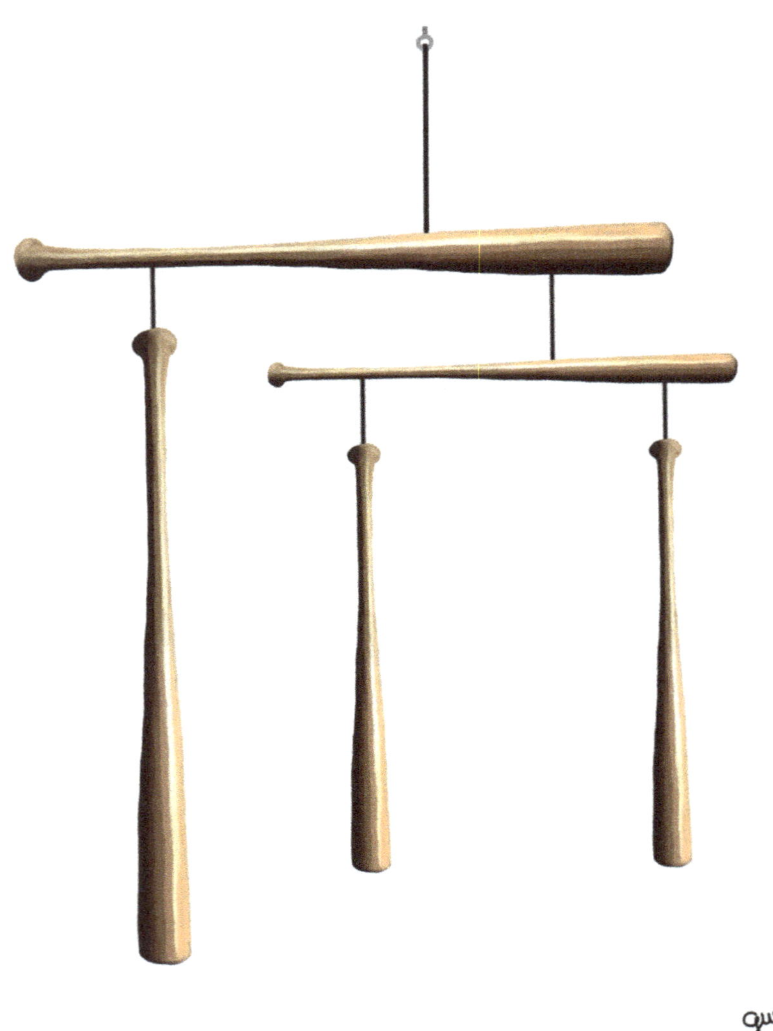

Bat Mobile

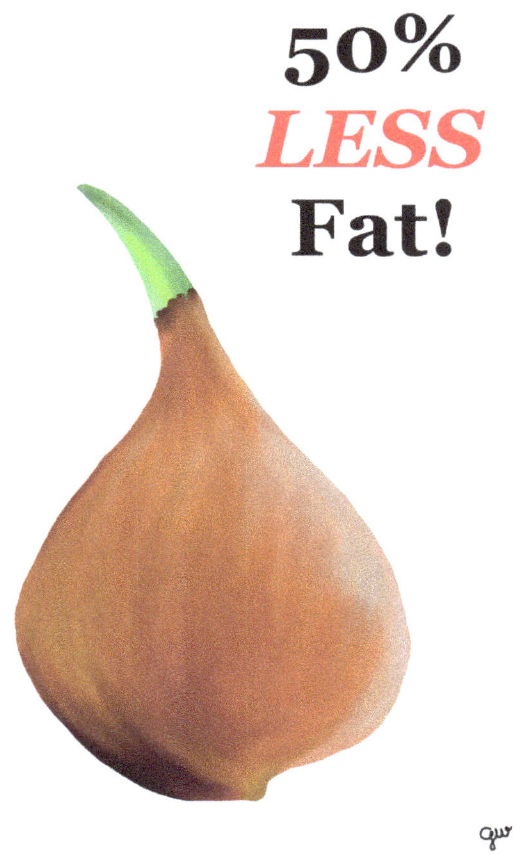

Lite Bulb

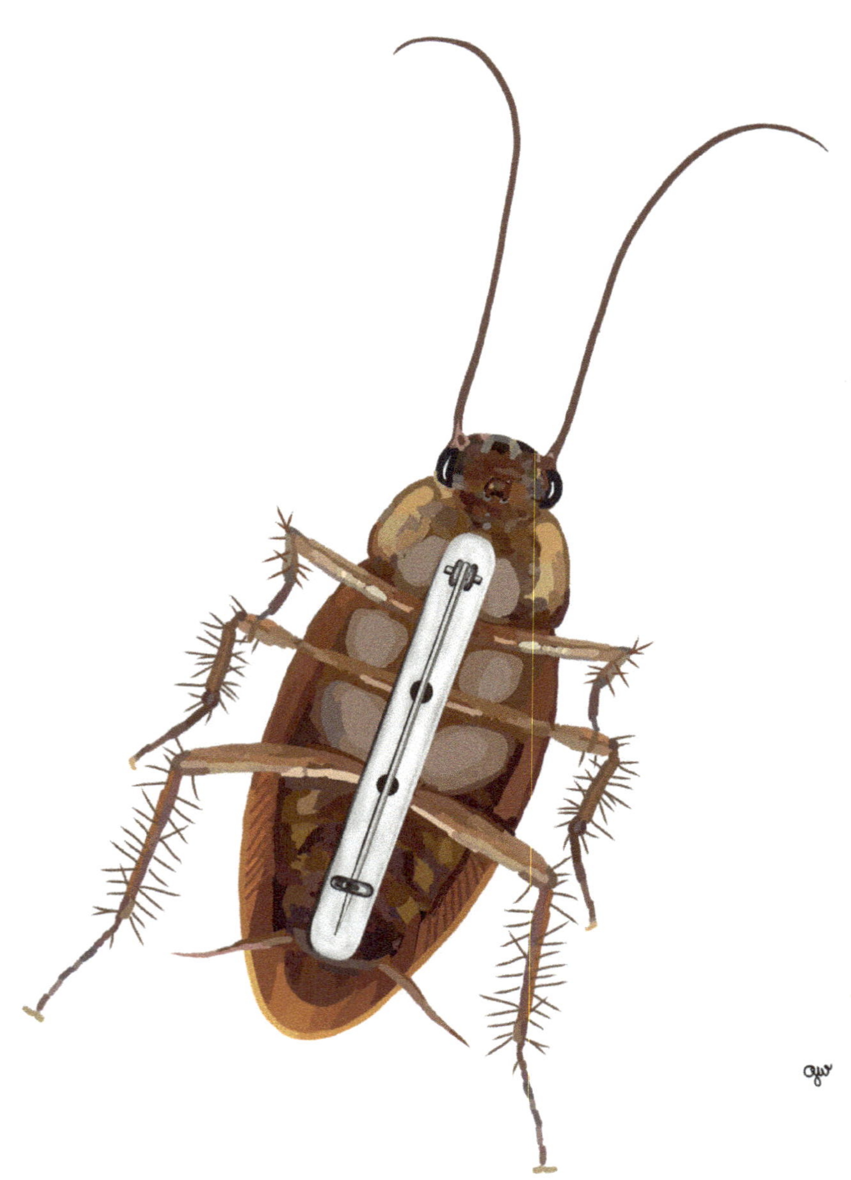

Broach

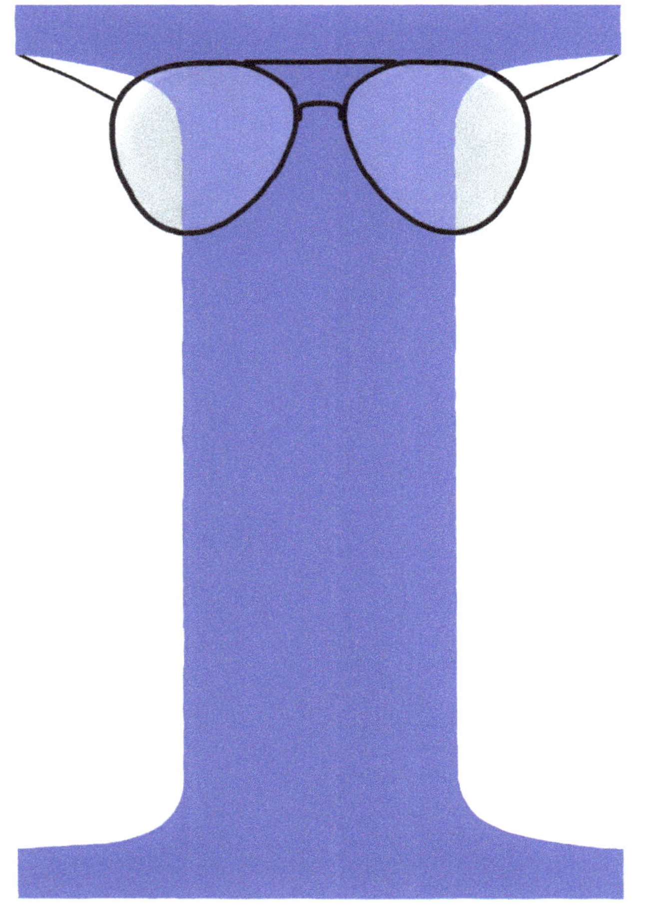

I Glasses

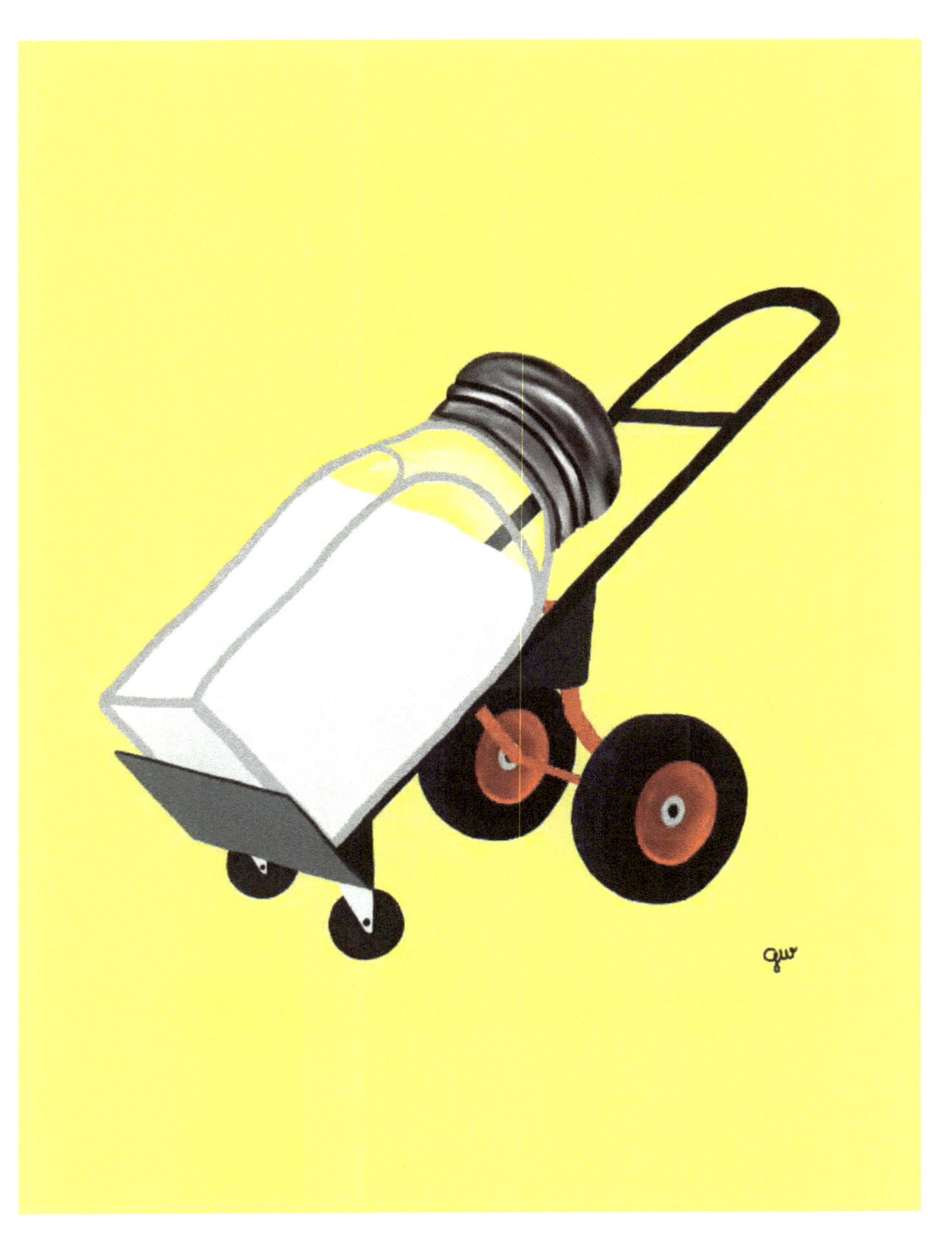

Mover and Shaker

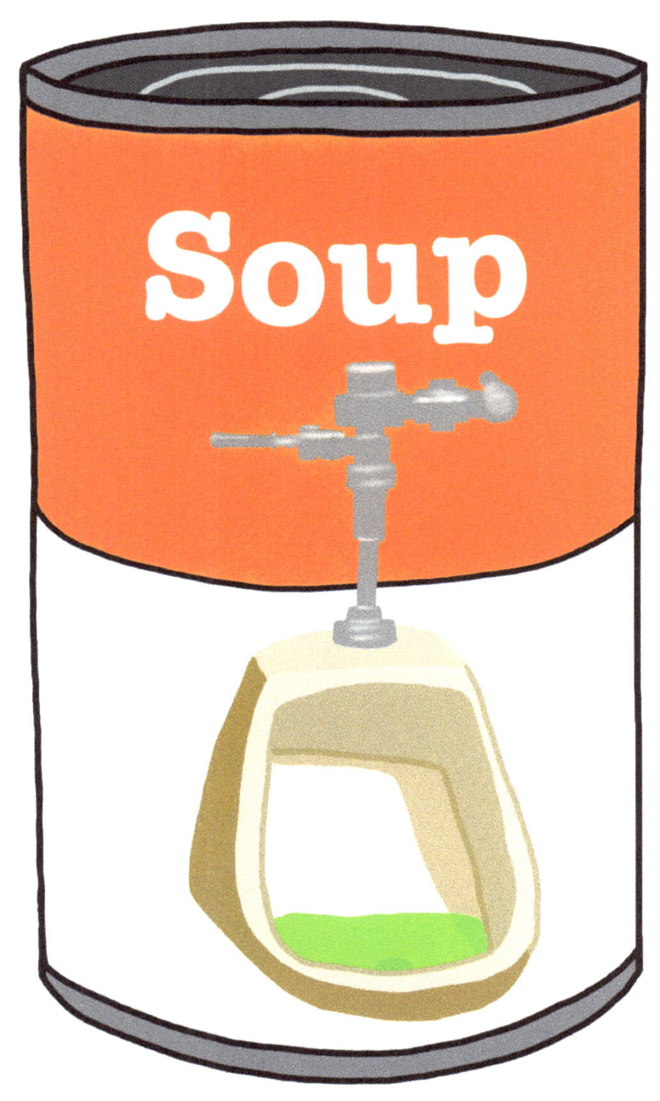

gw

Green Pee

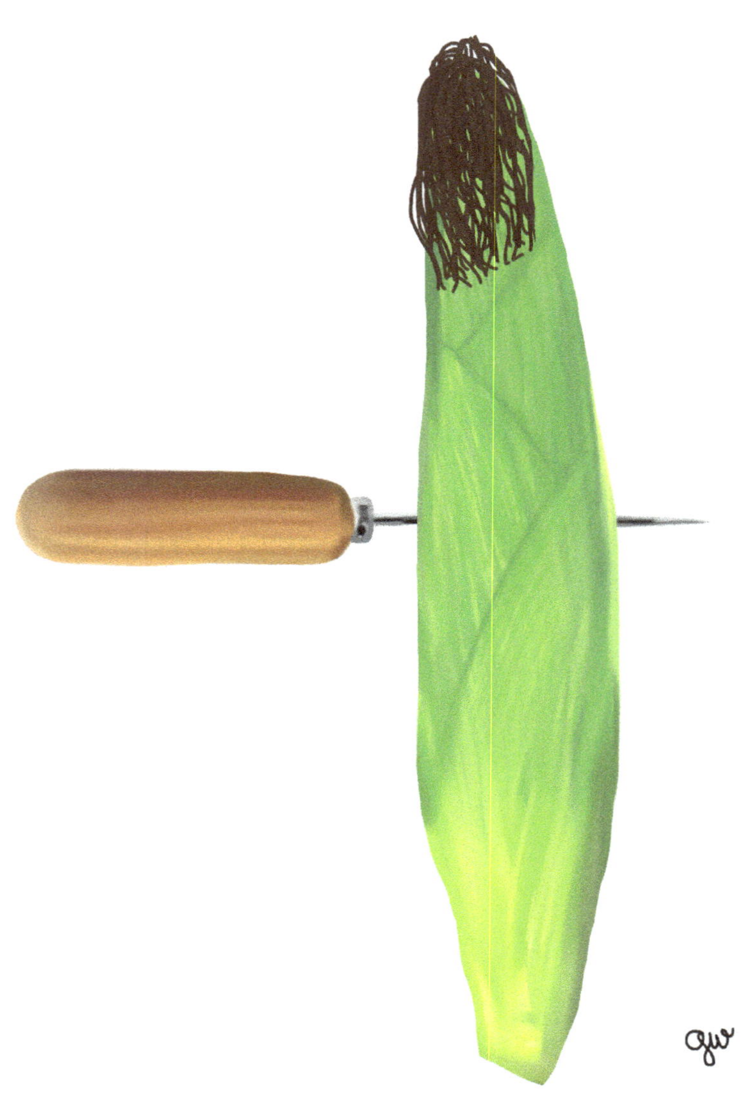

Pierced Ear

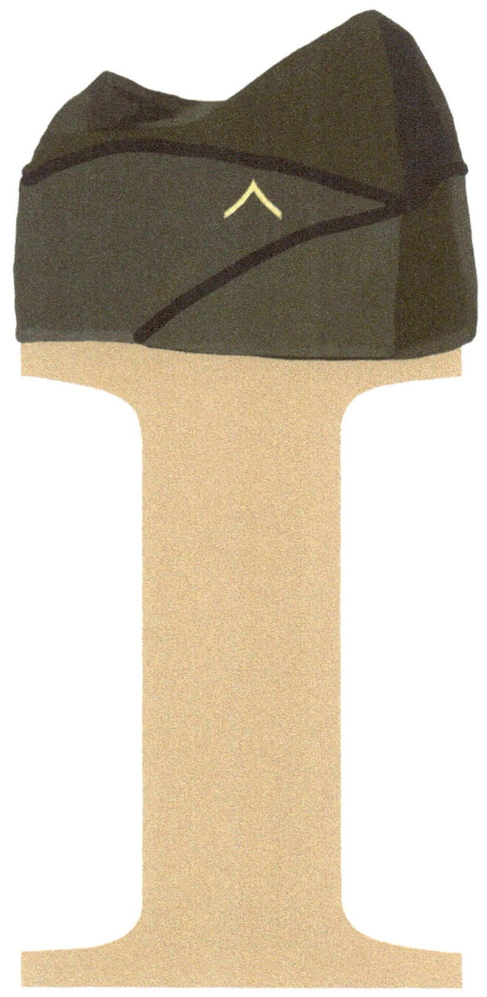

Private I

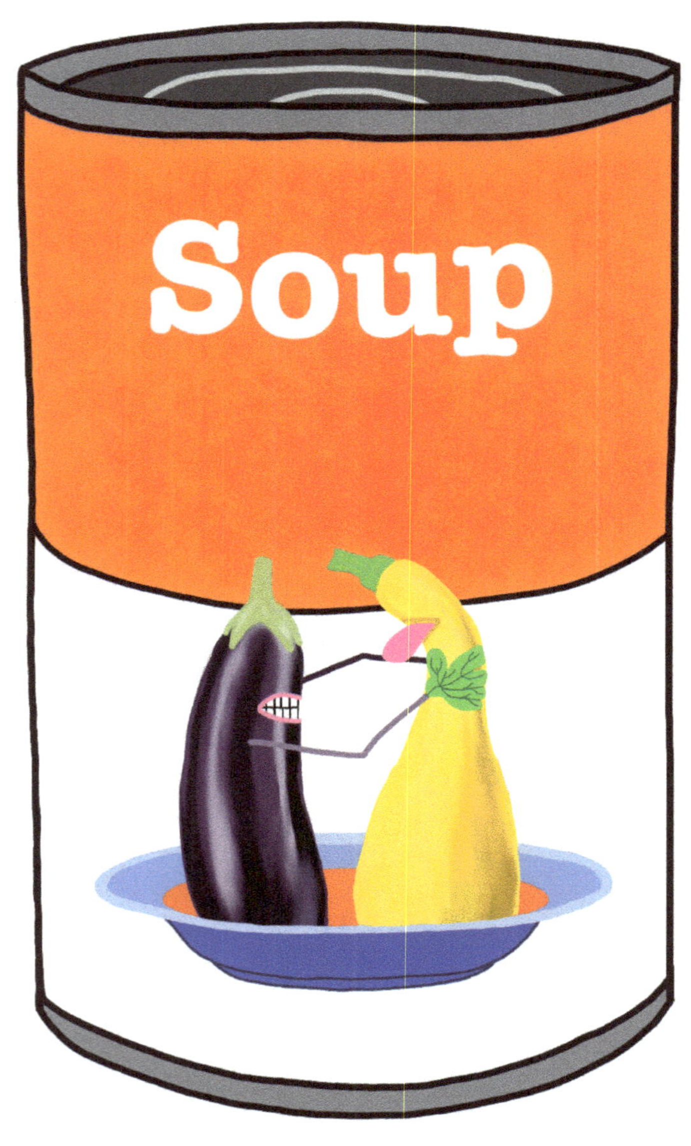

gw

Vegetable Beef

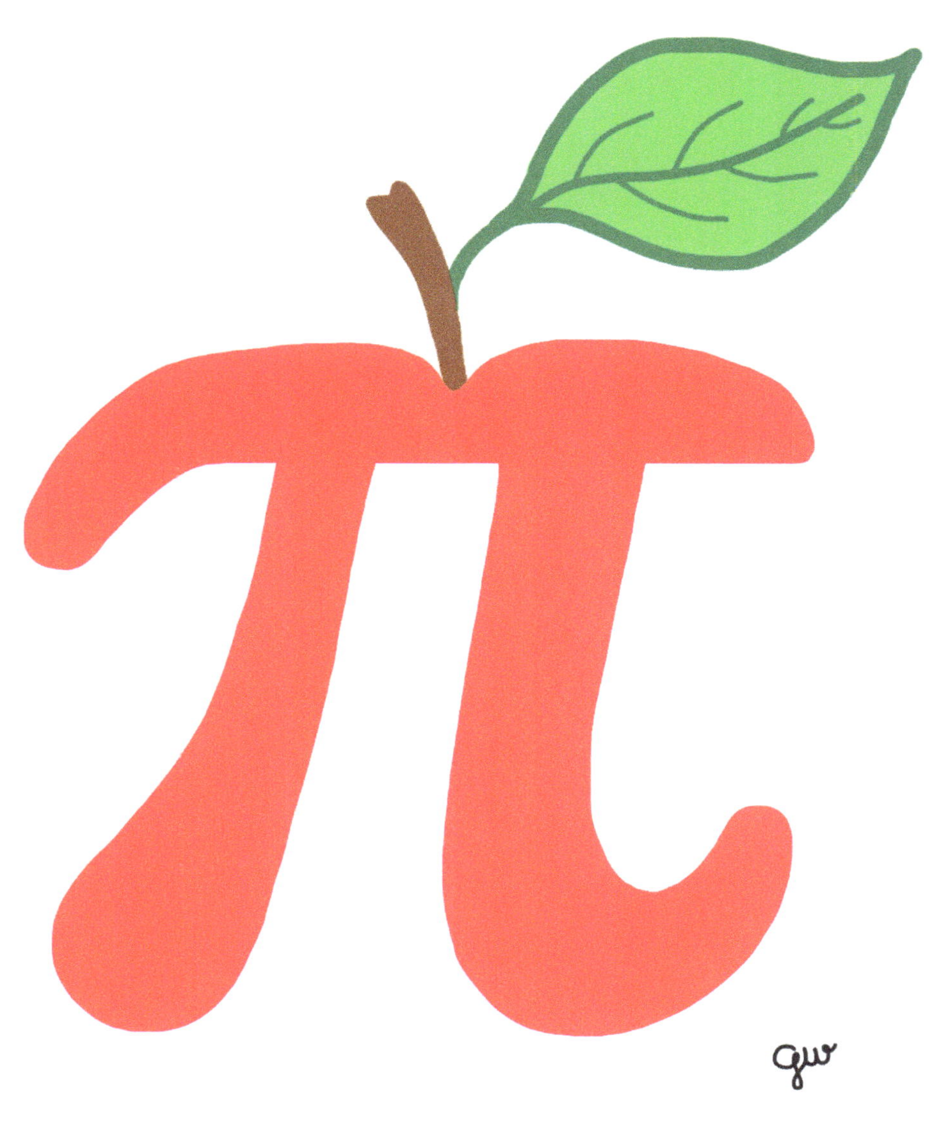

Apple Pi

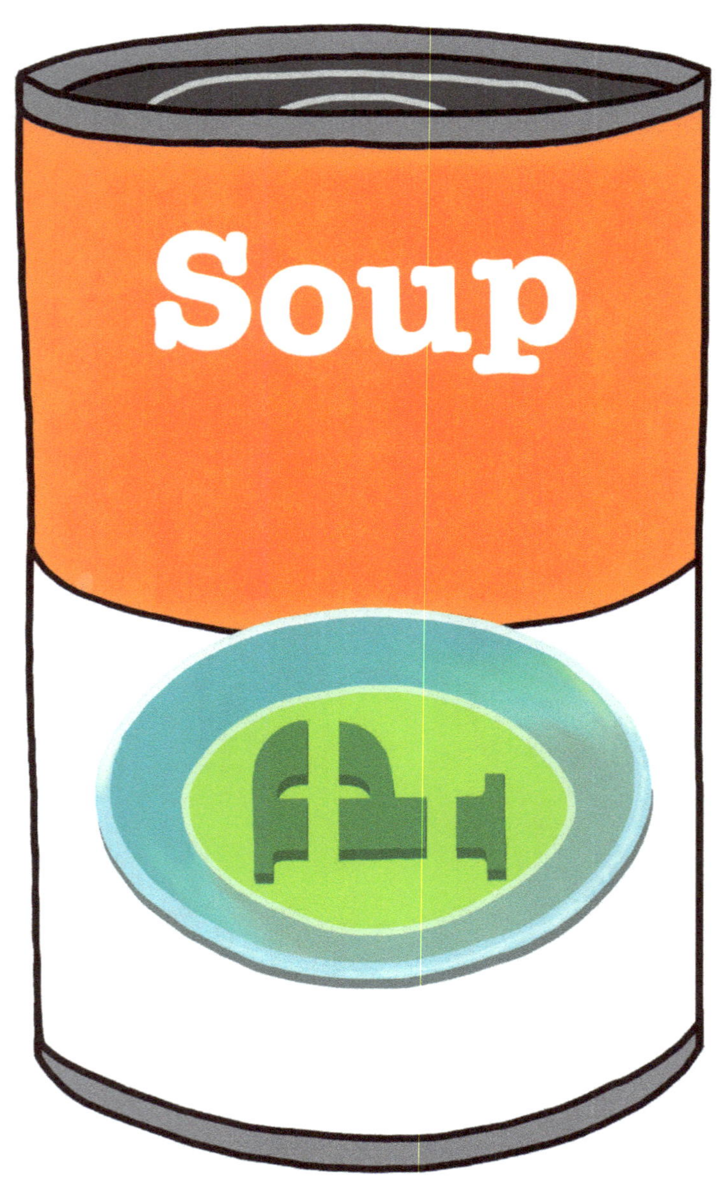

Split P

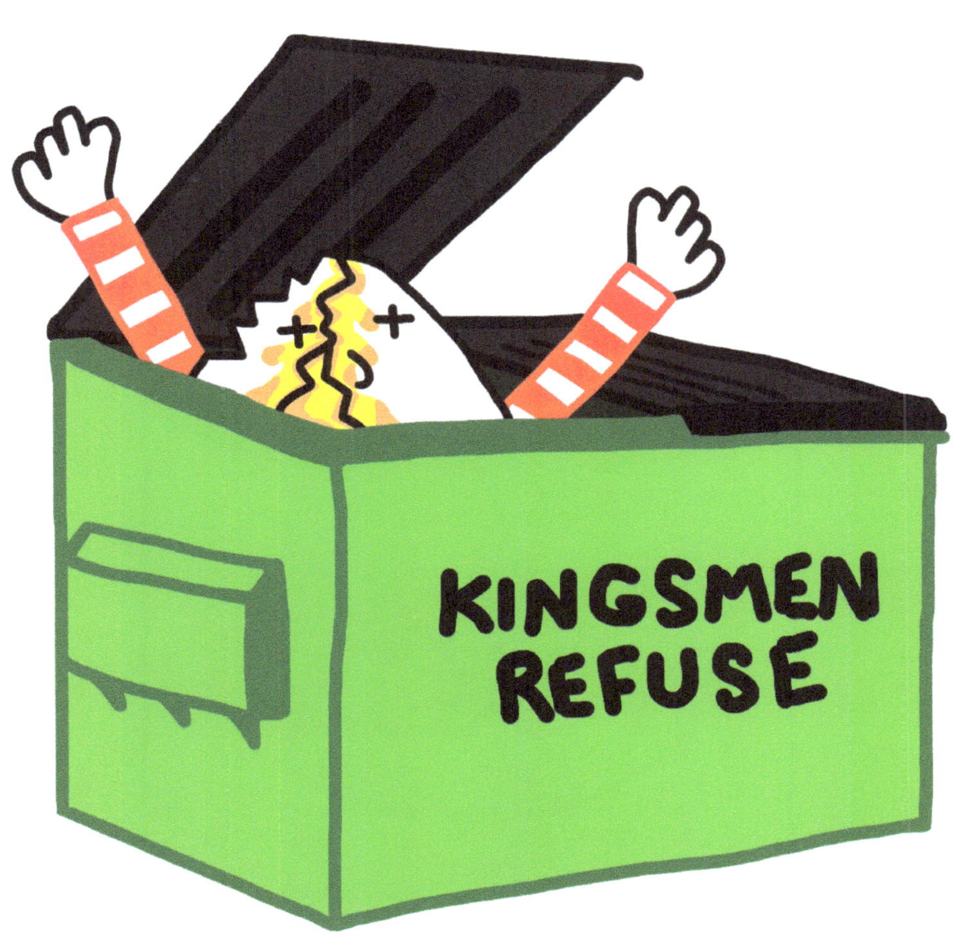

Humpty Dumpster

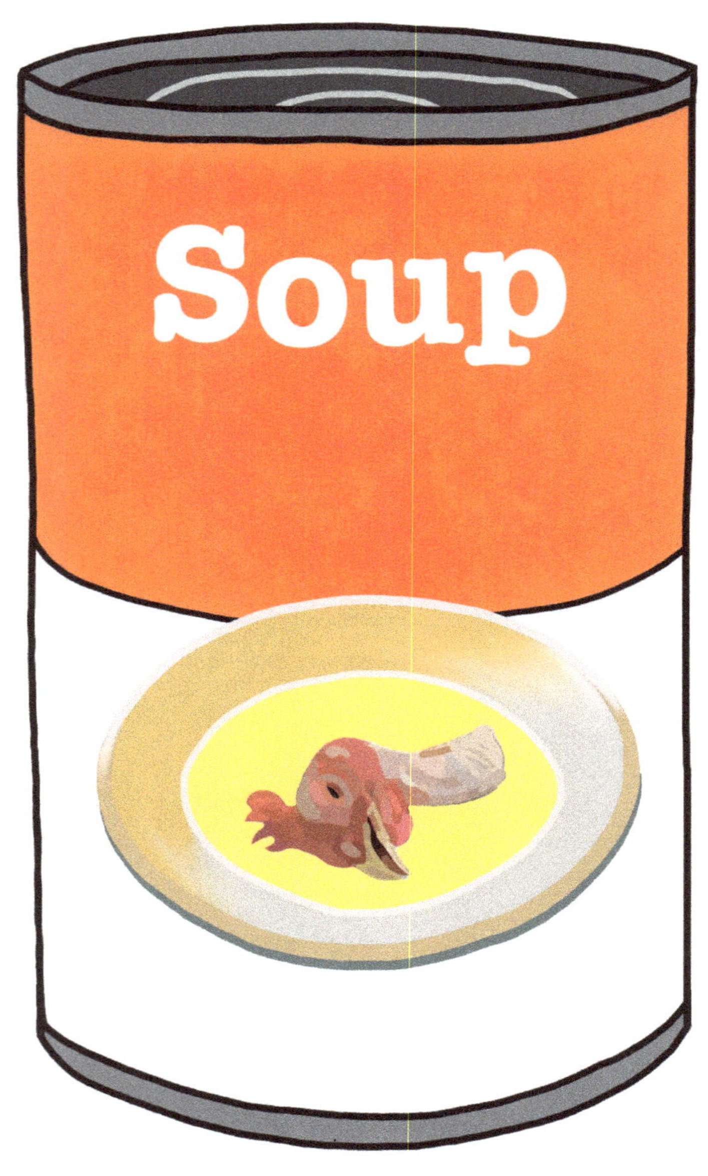

Chicken Noodle

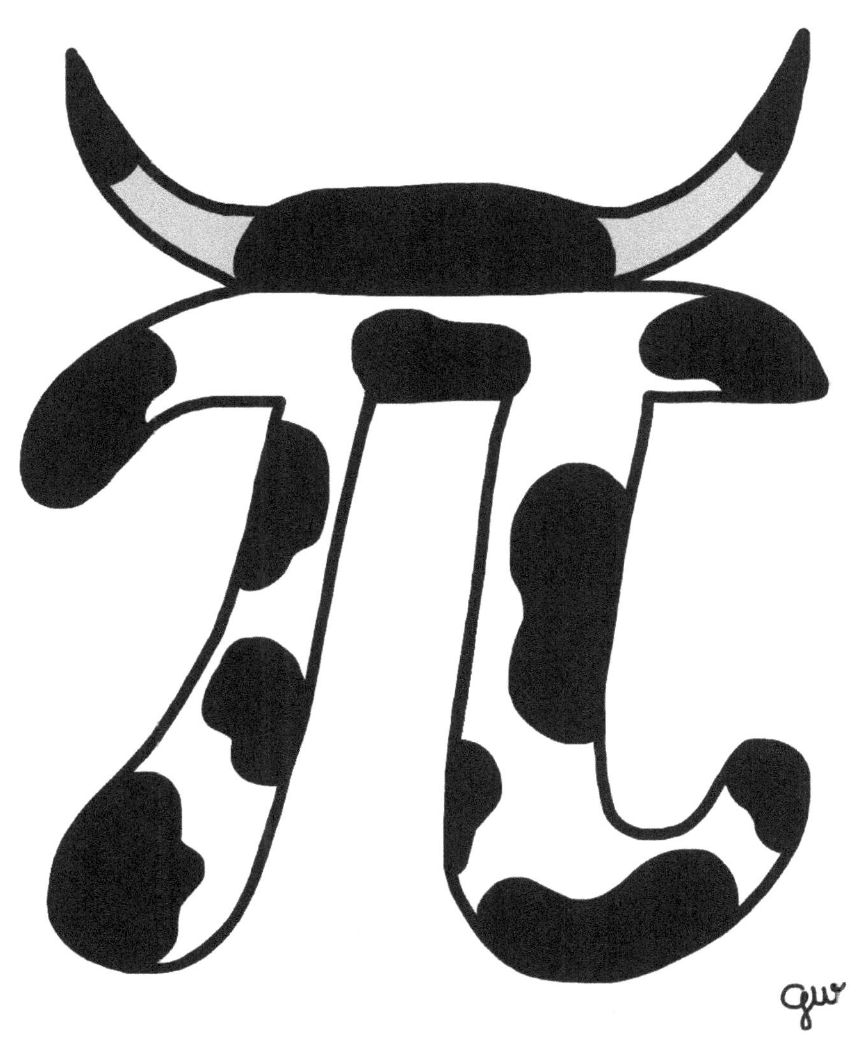

Cow Pi

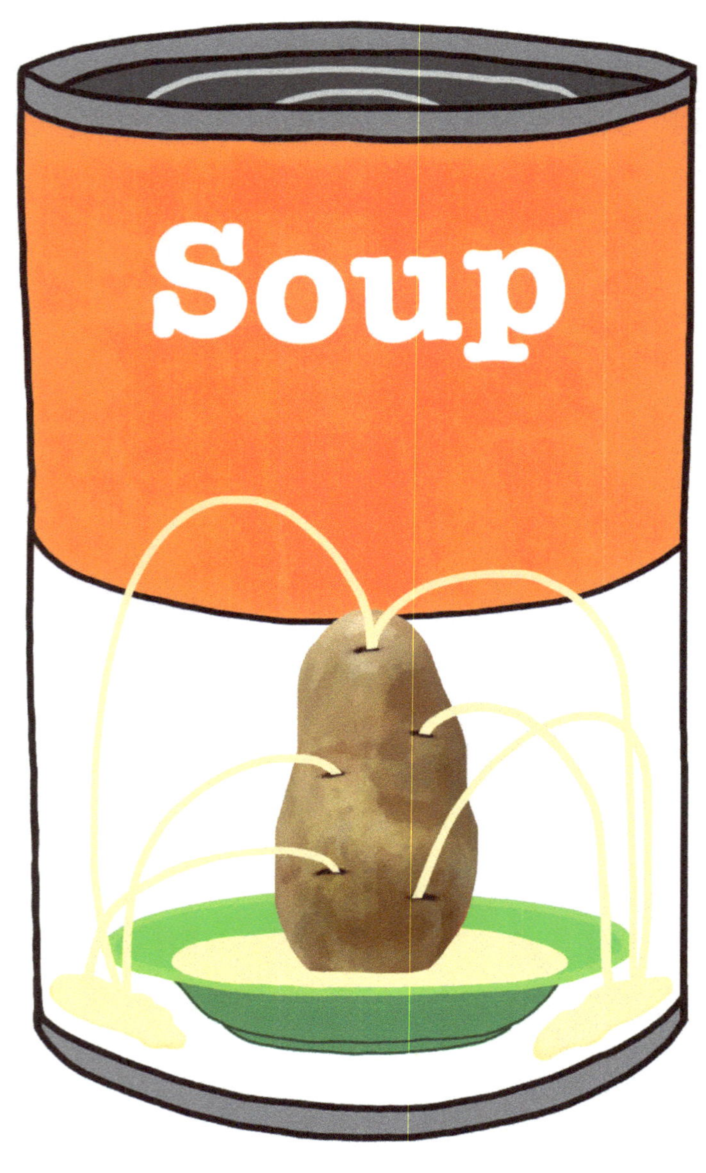

gw

Potato Leak

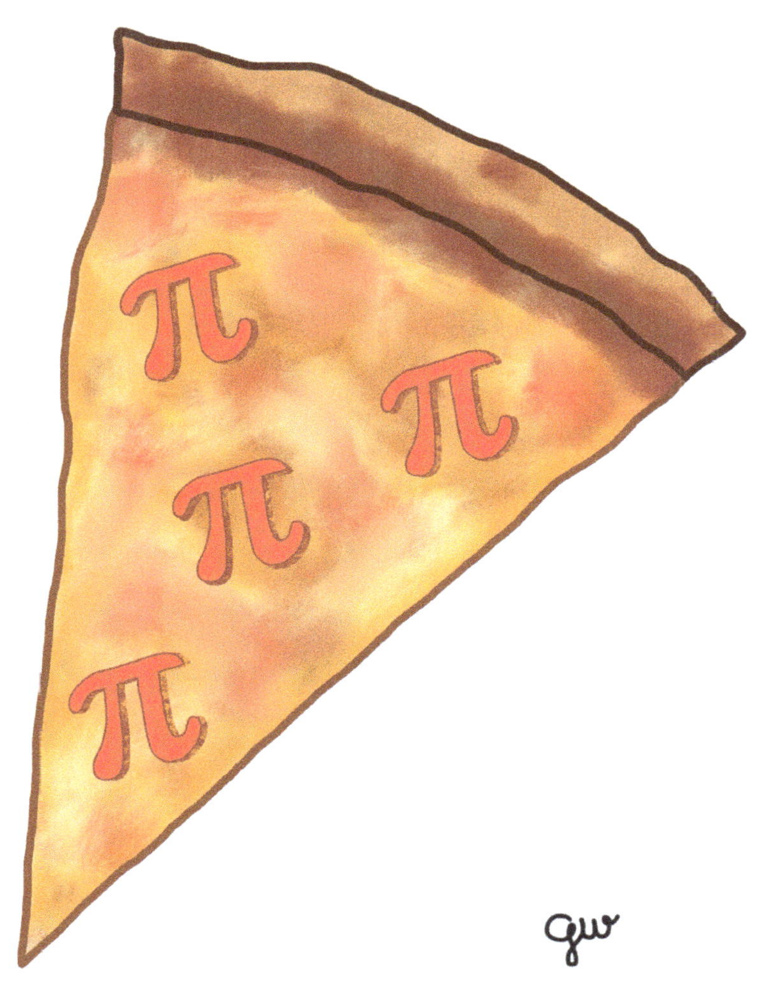

Pizza Pi

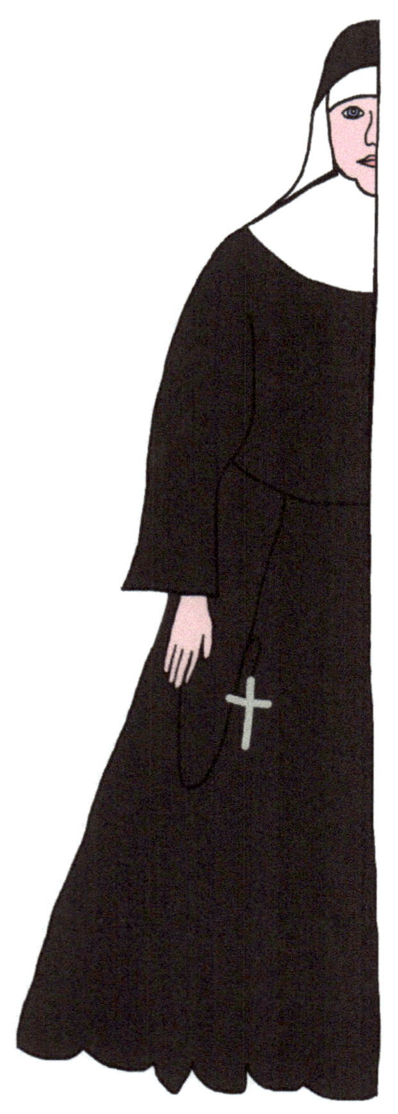

Half Sister

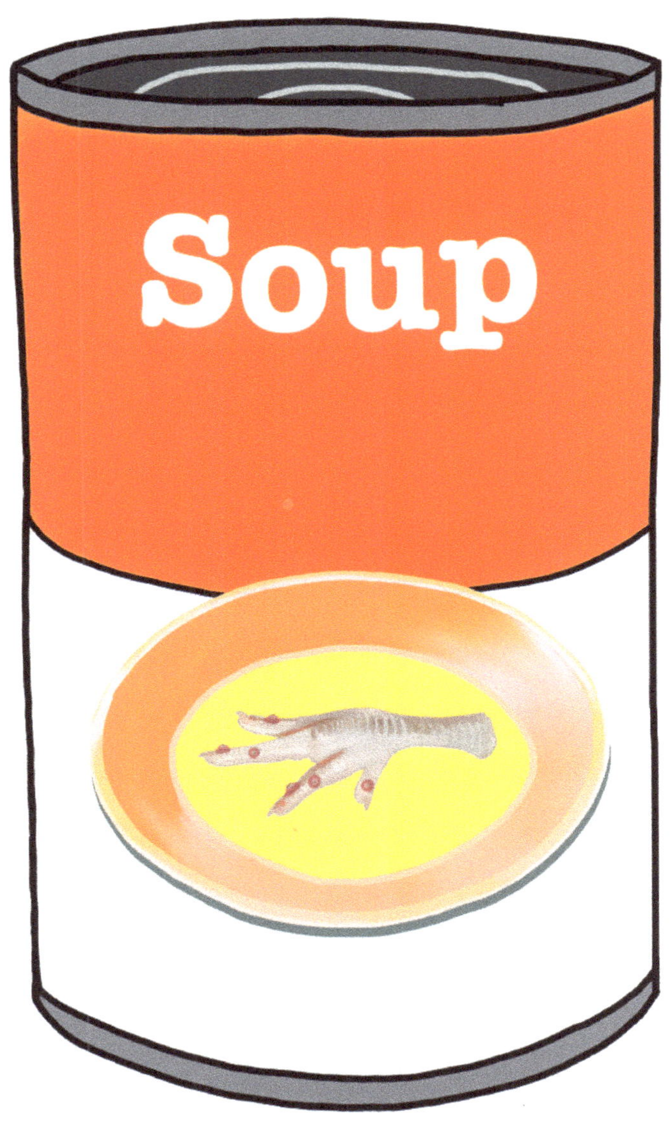

gw

Chicken Corn

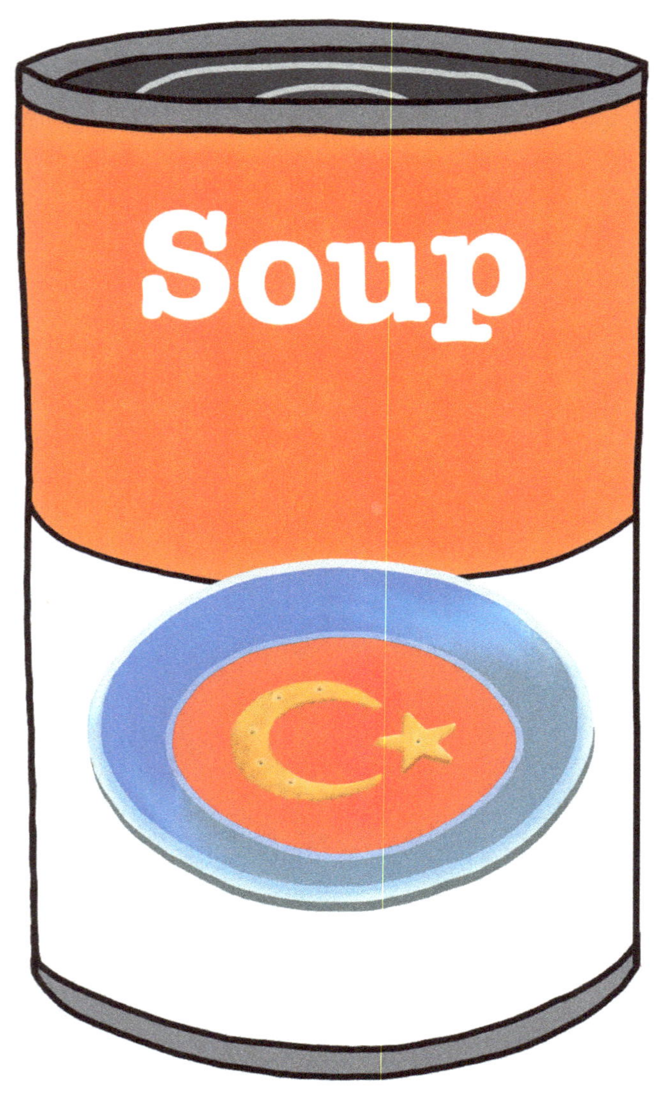

Turkey

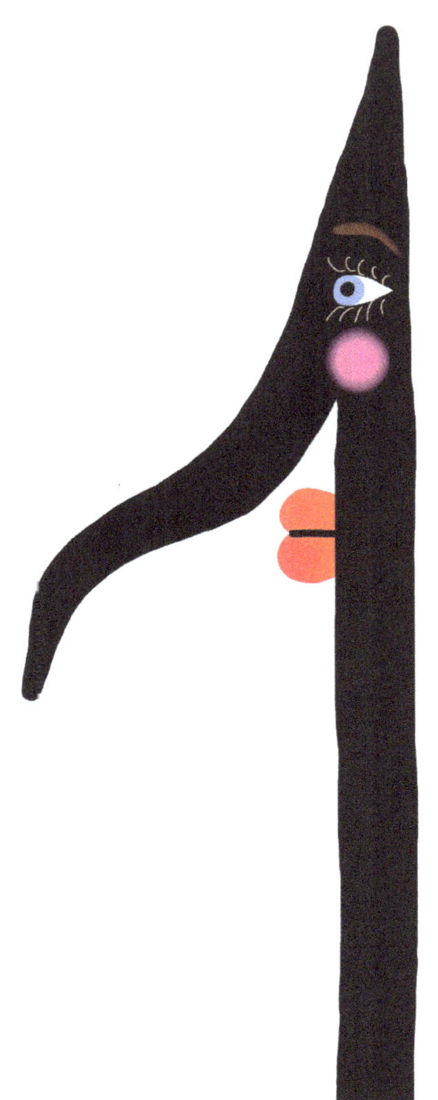

Poker Face

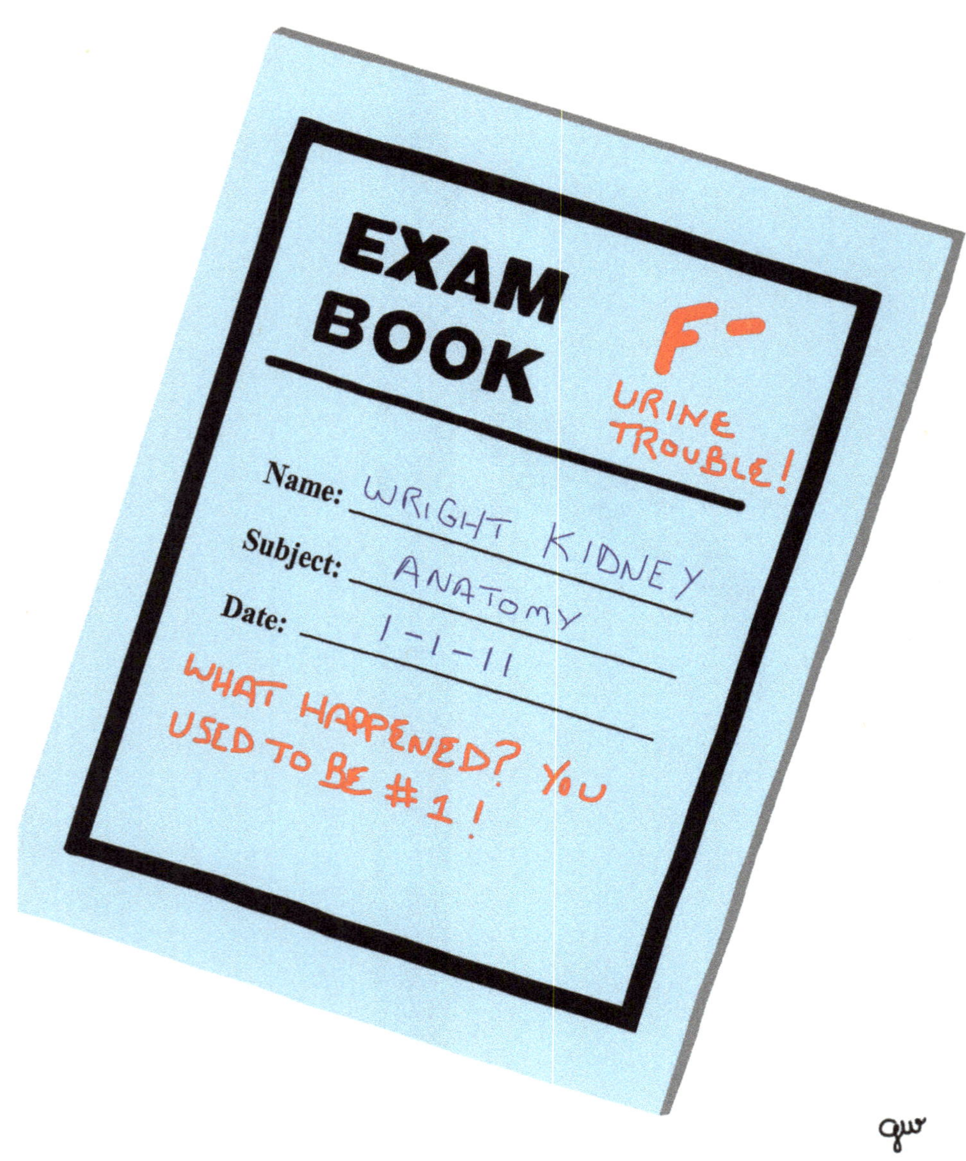

Renal Failure

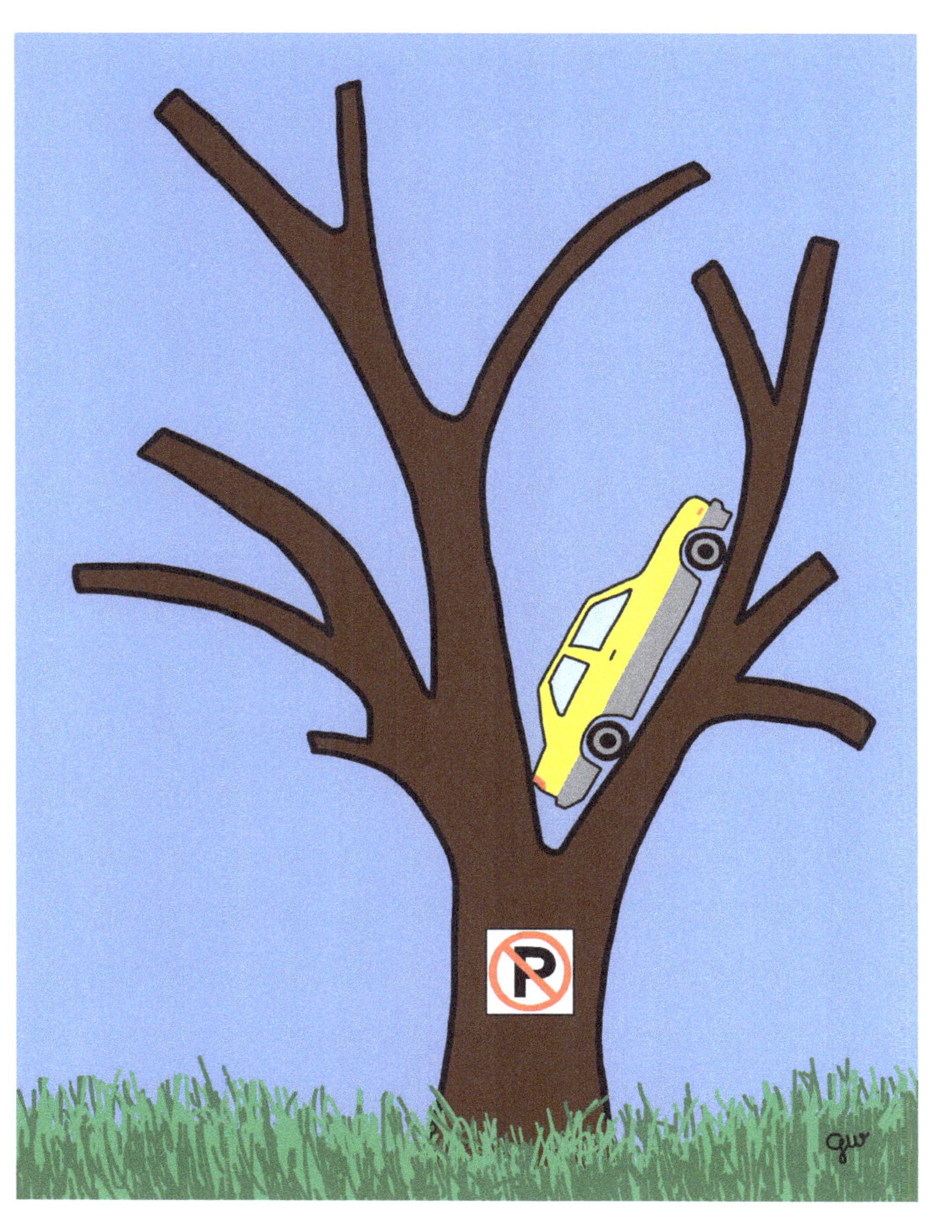

Parking Up
The Wrong Tree

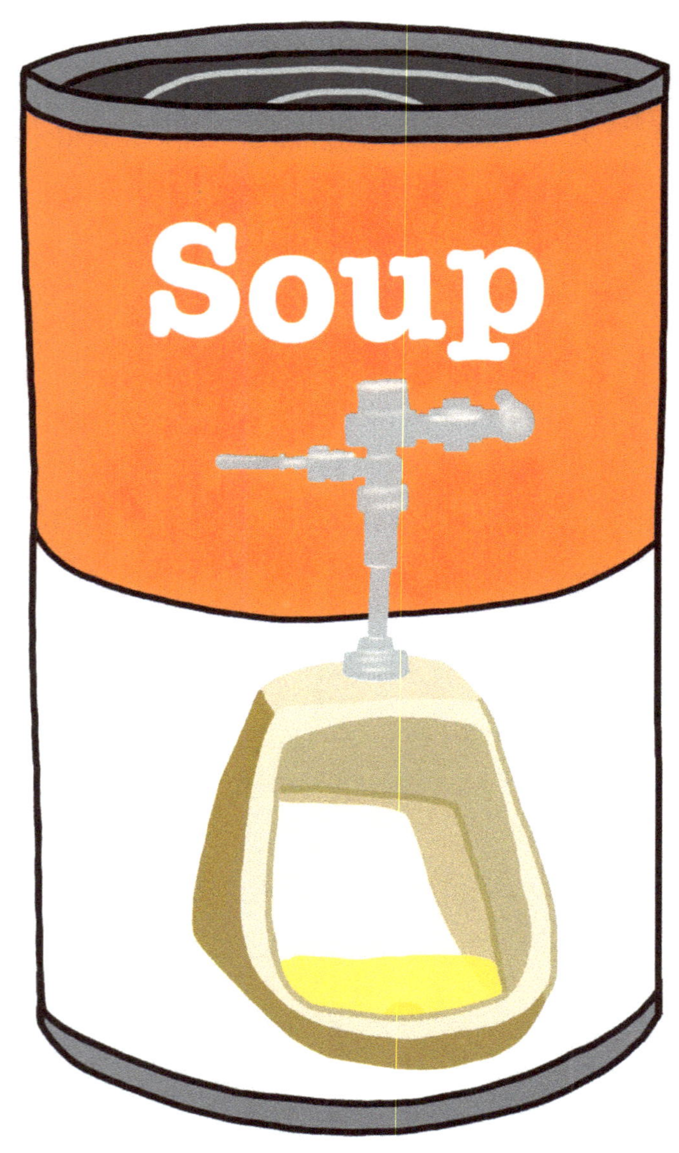

gw

Leak

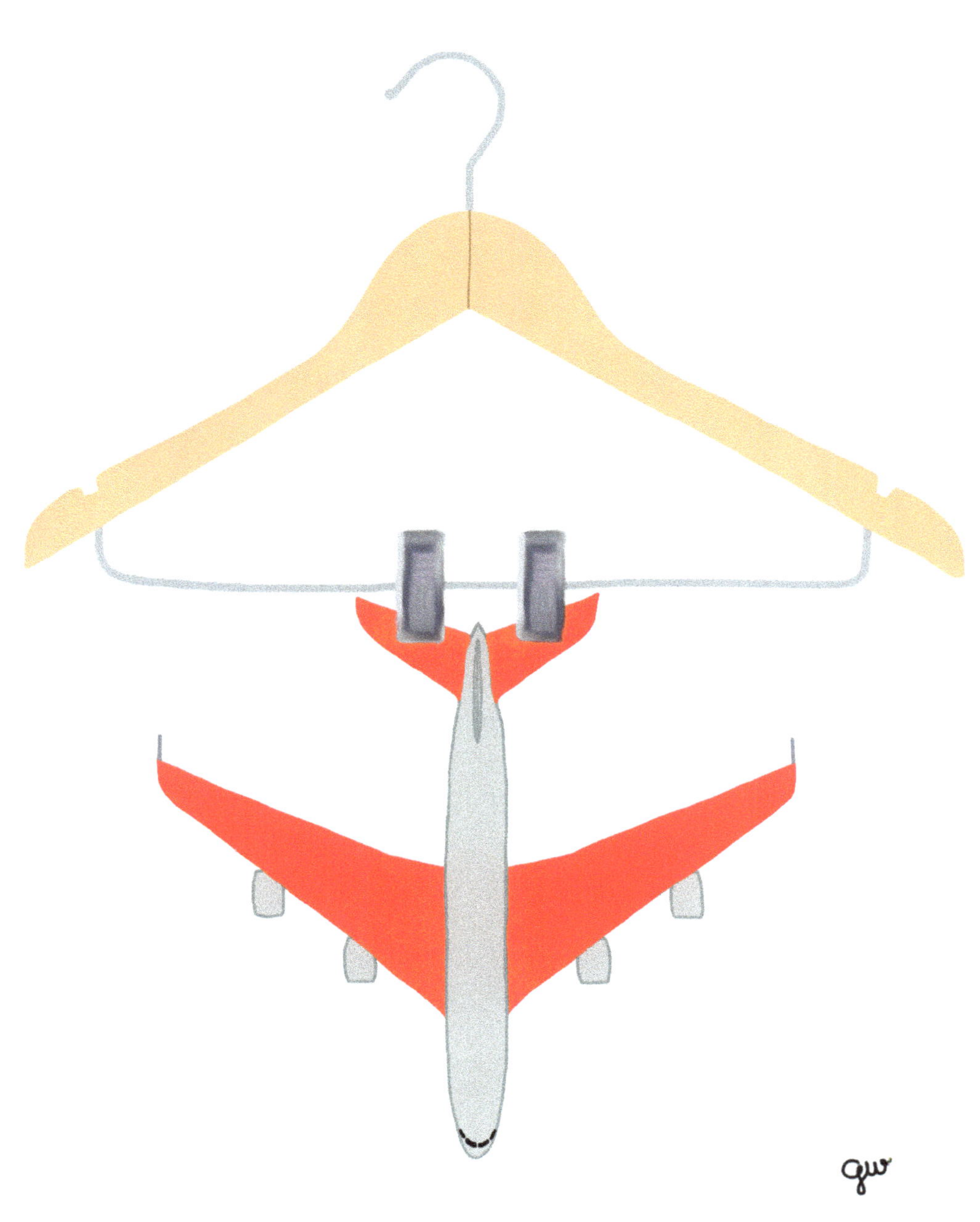

Airplane Hanger

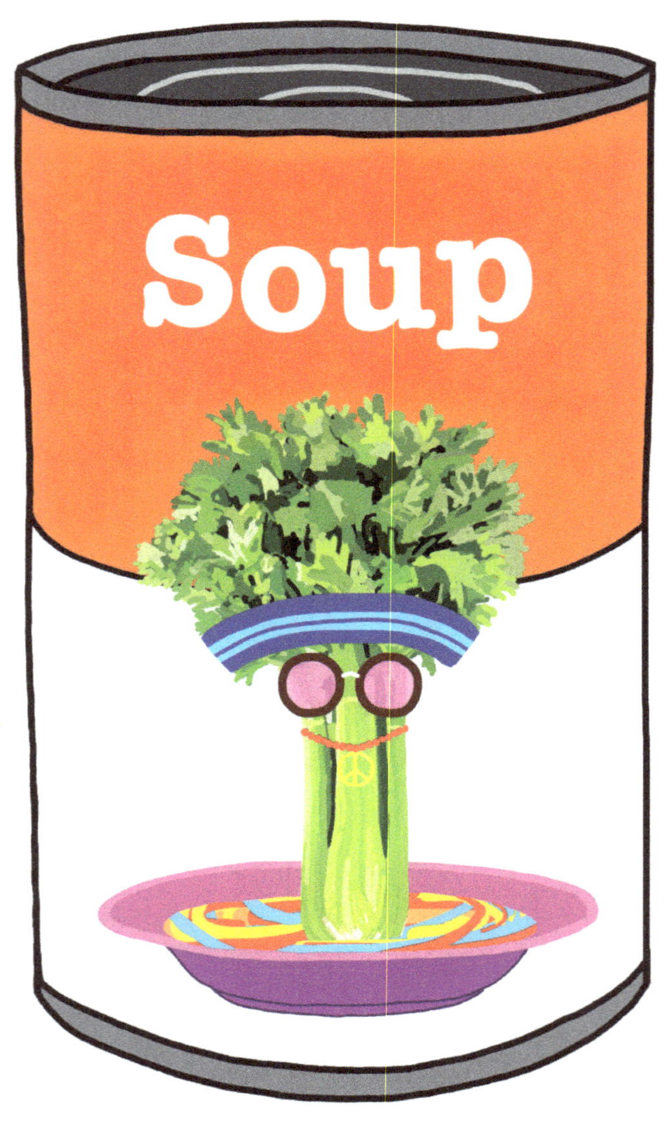

gw

Vegetarian Vegetable

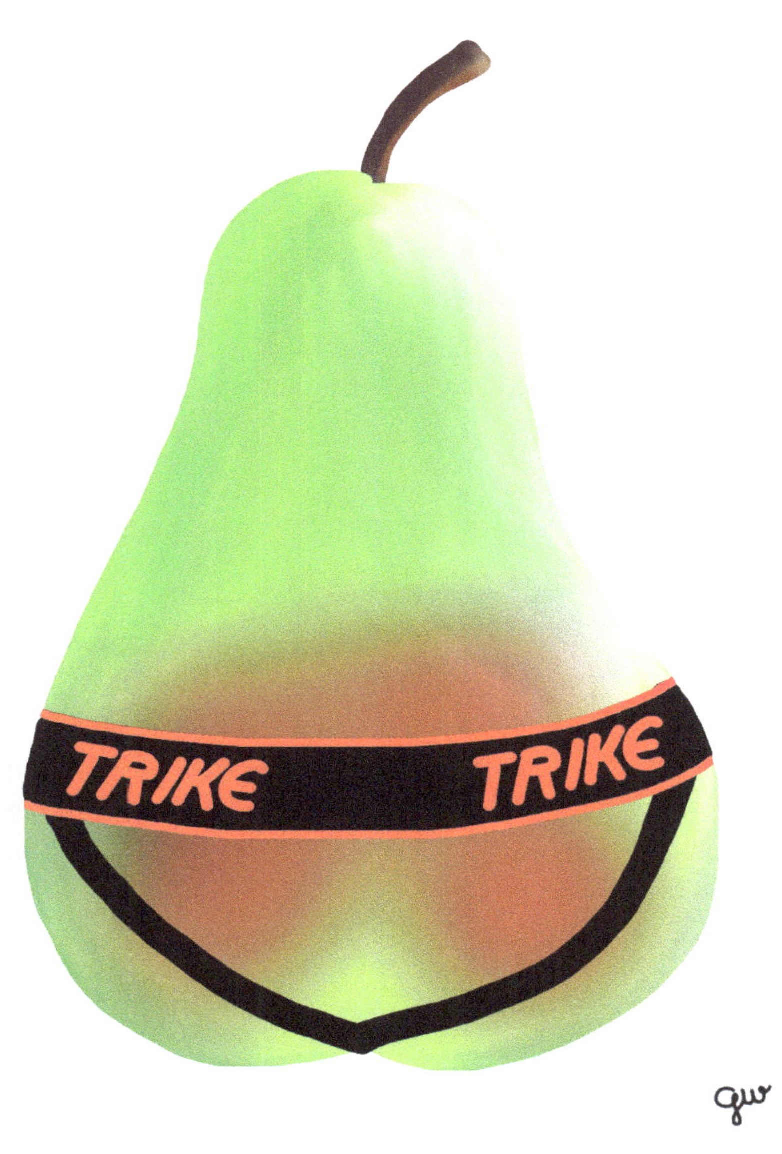

Fruit Cup (rear view)

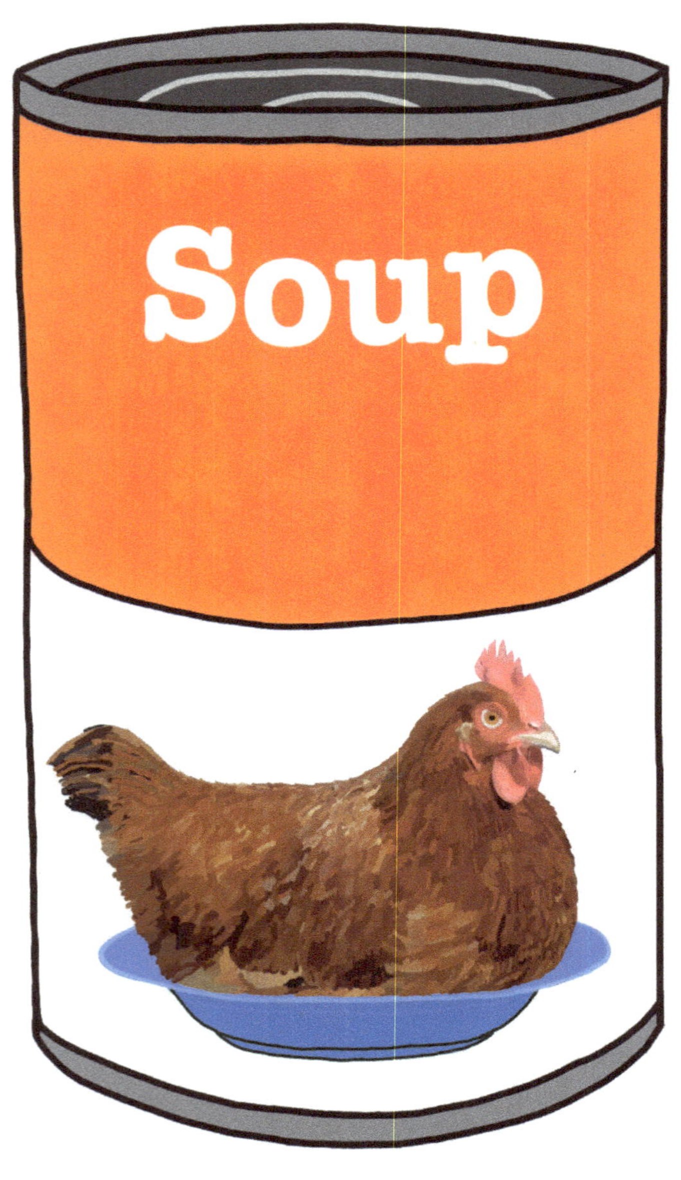

gw

Egg Plant

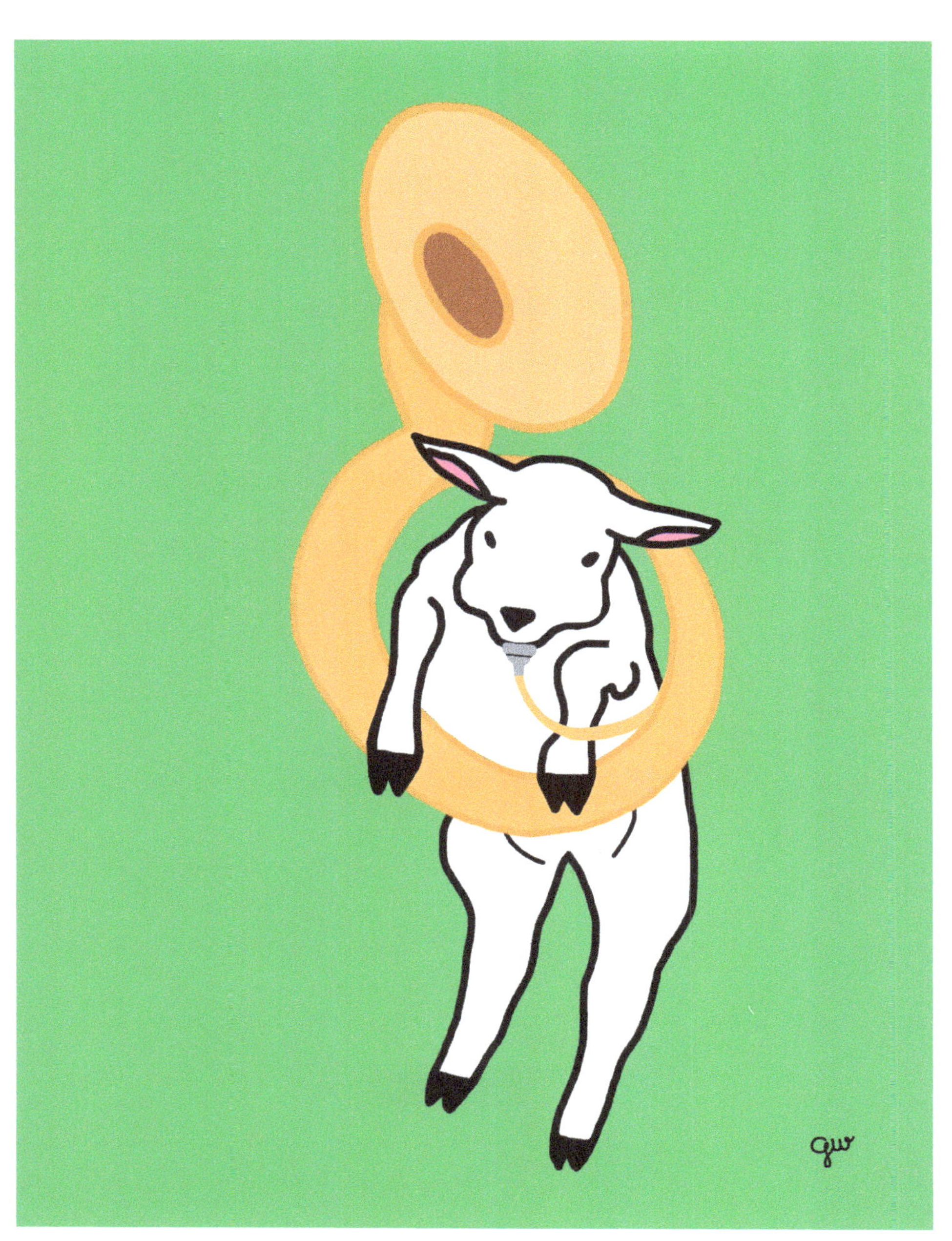

Big Horn Sheep

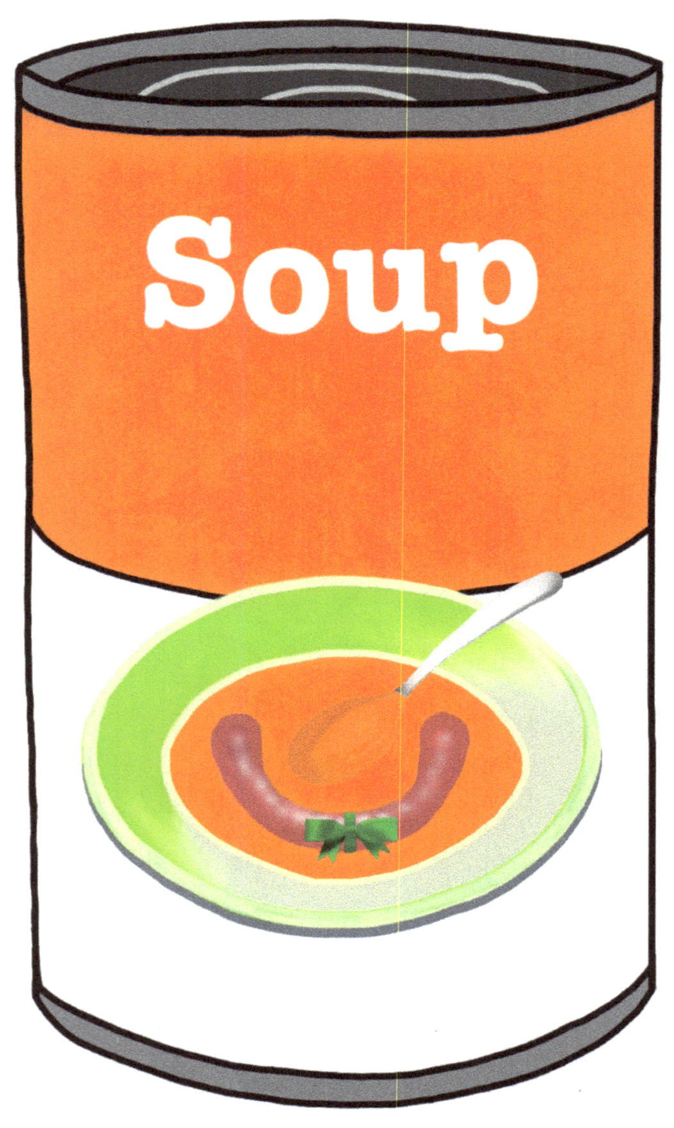

gw

Gum Bow

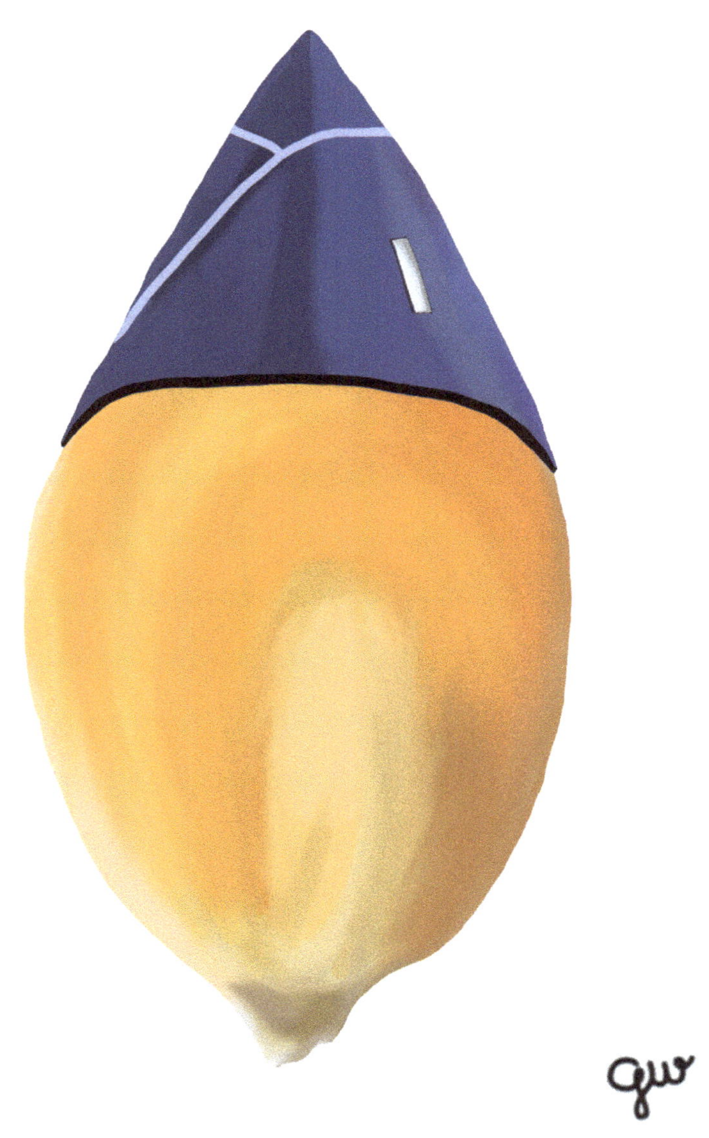

Lieutenant Kernel

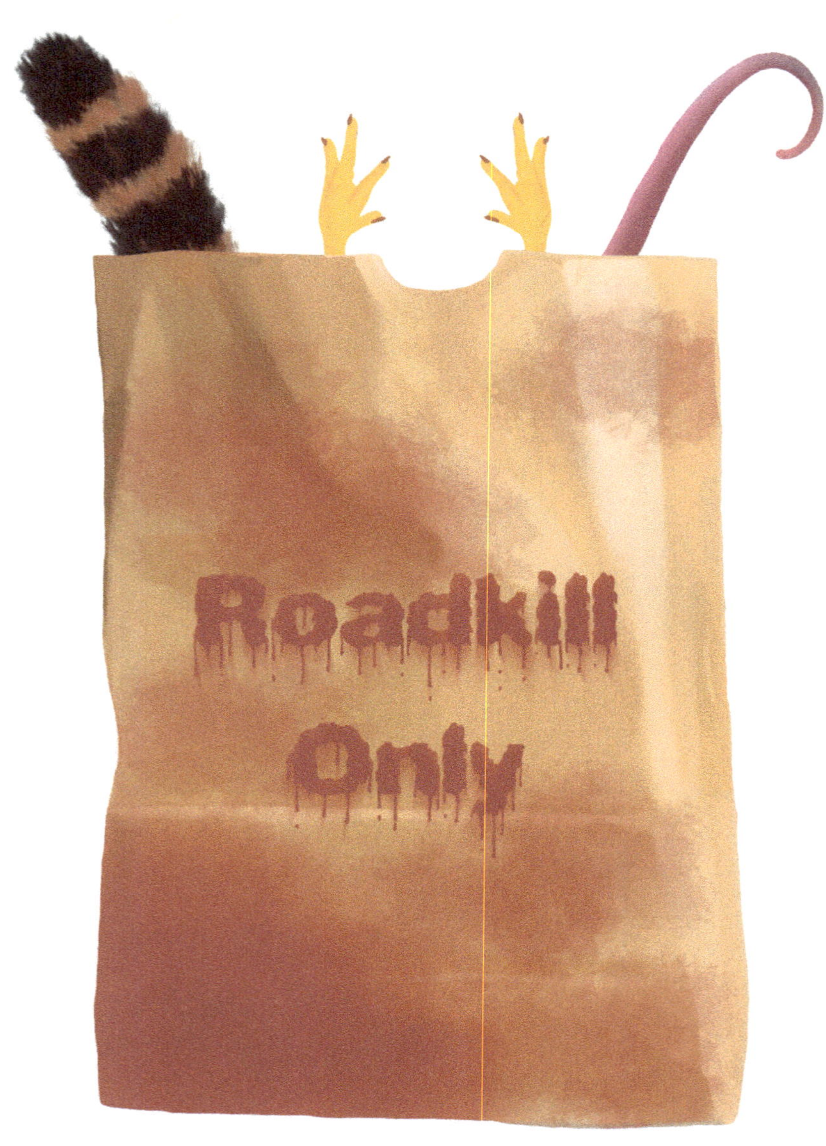

Carrion Bag

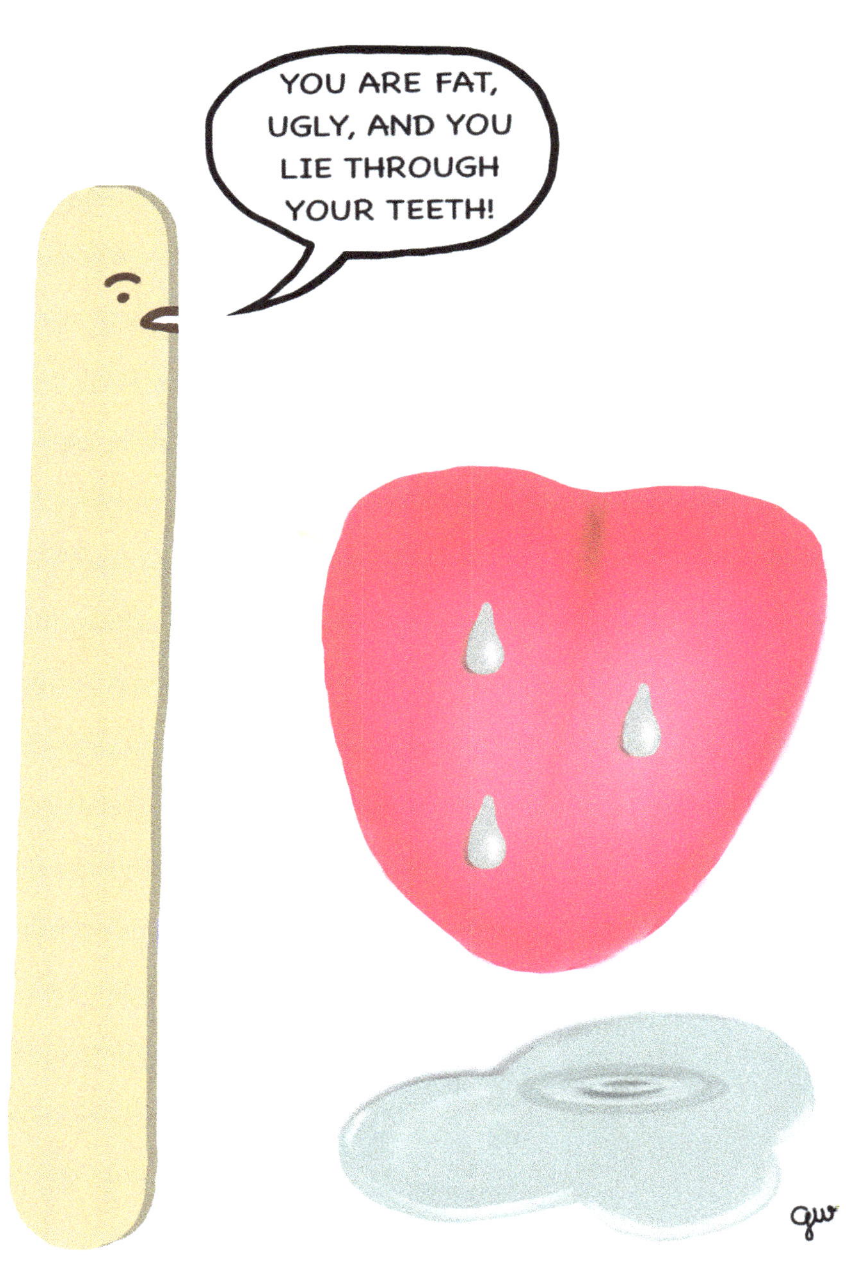

Tongue Depresser

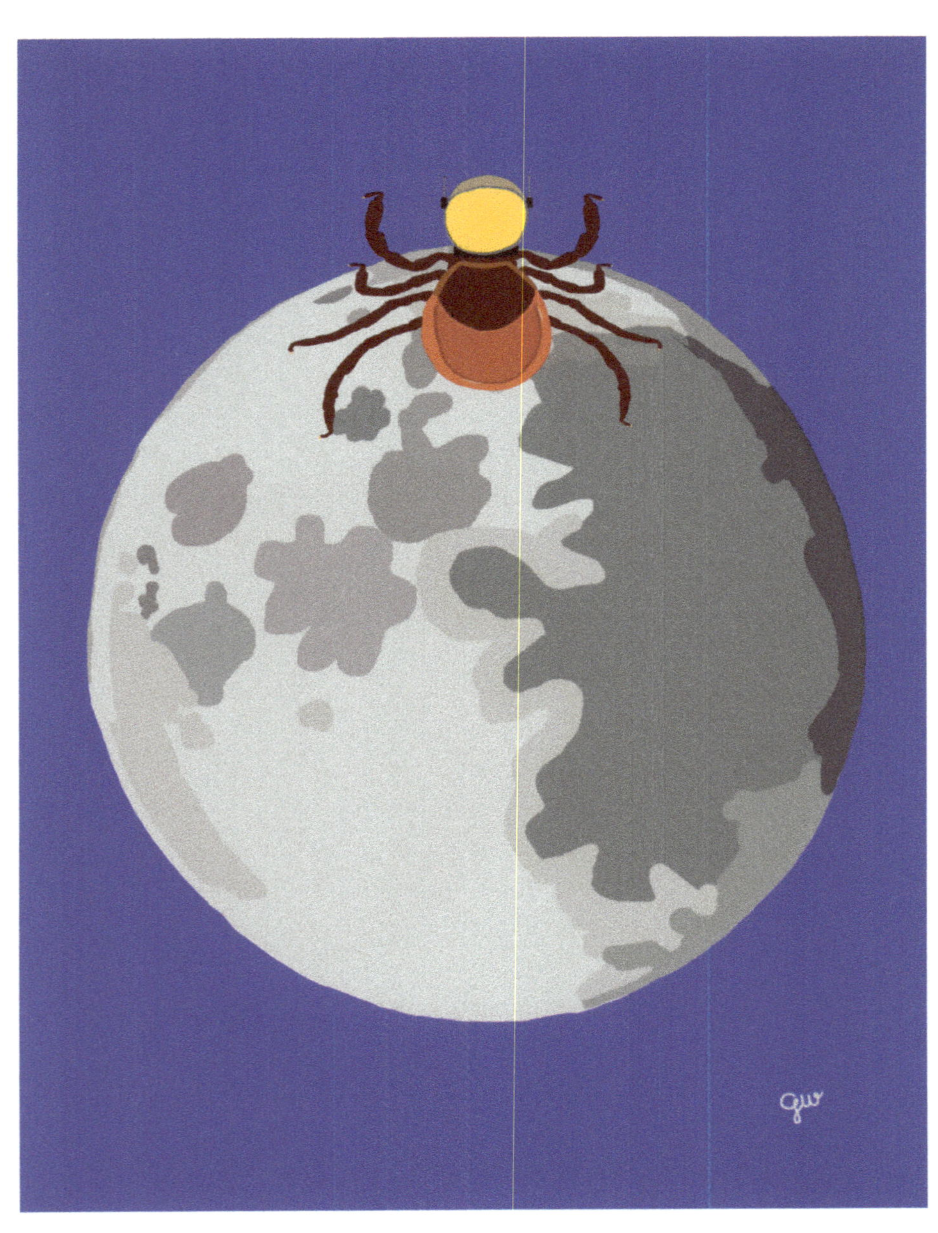

Lunar Tick

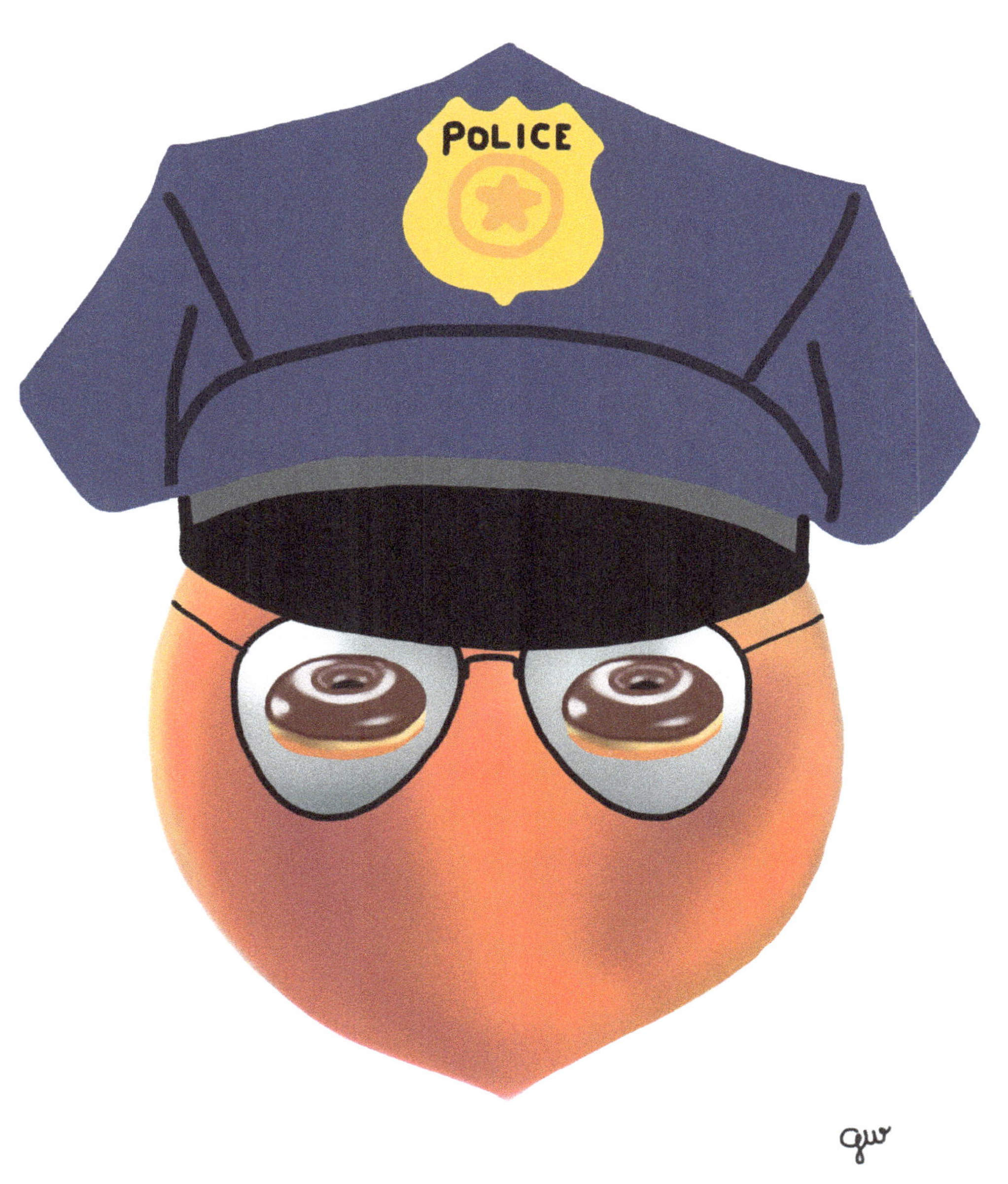

Peach Fuzz

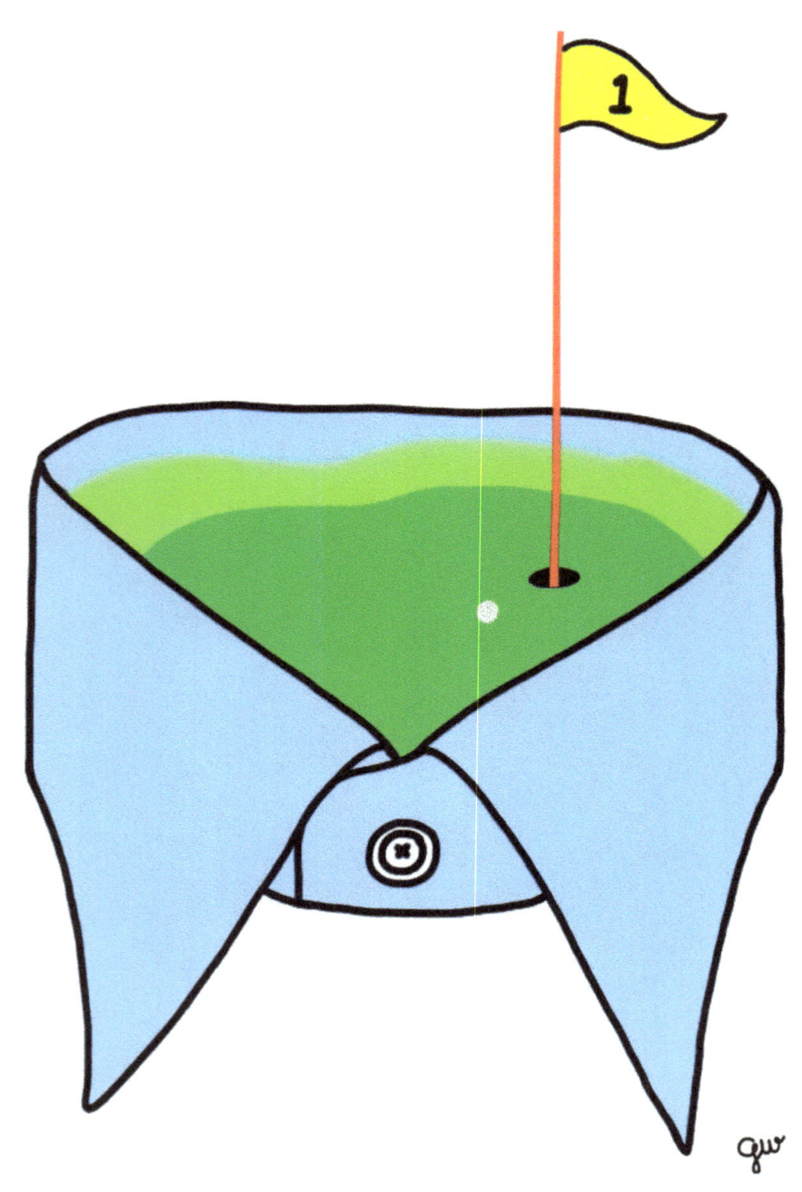

Collared Green

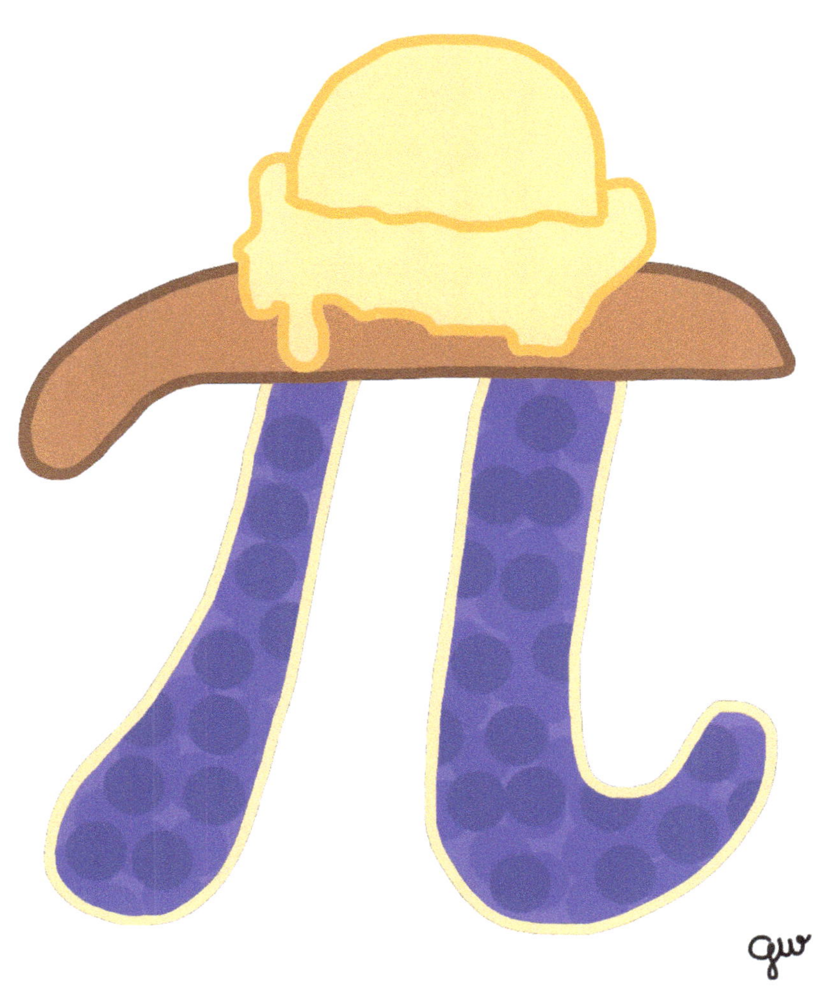

Pi a la Mode

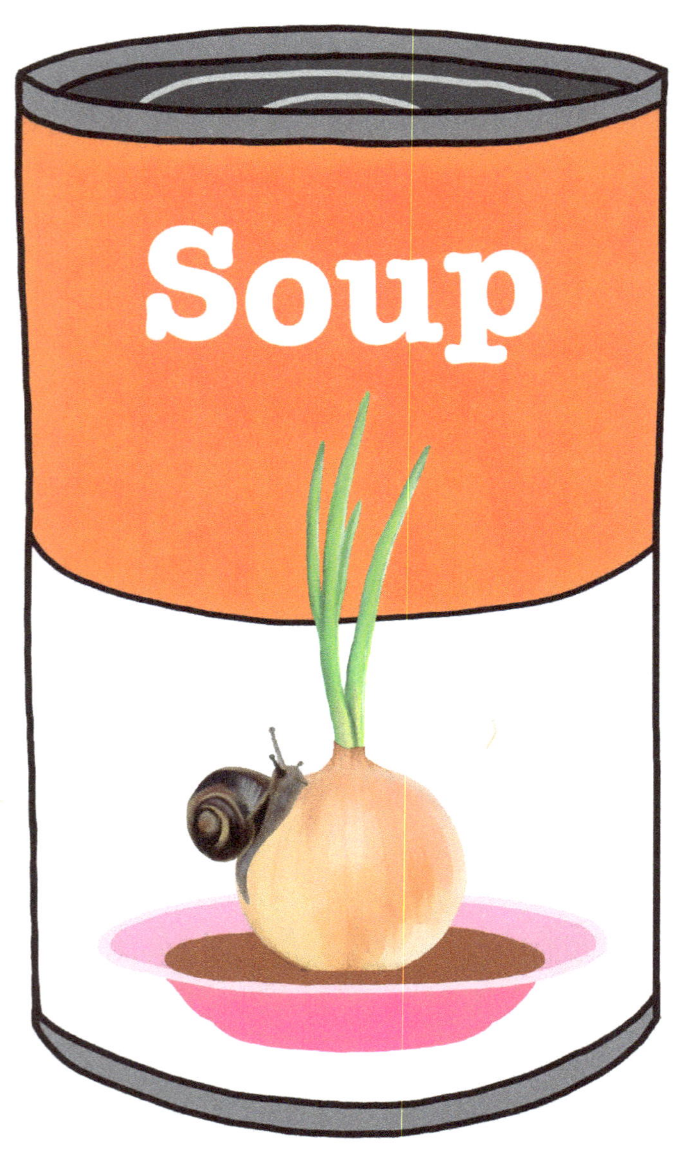

gw

French Onion

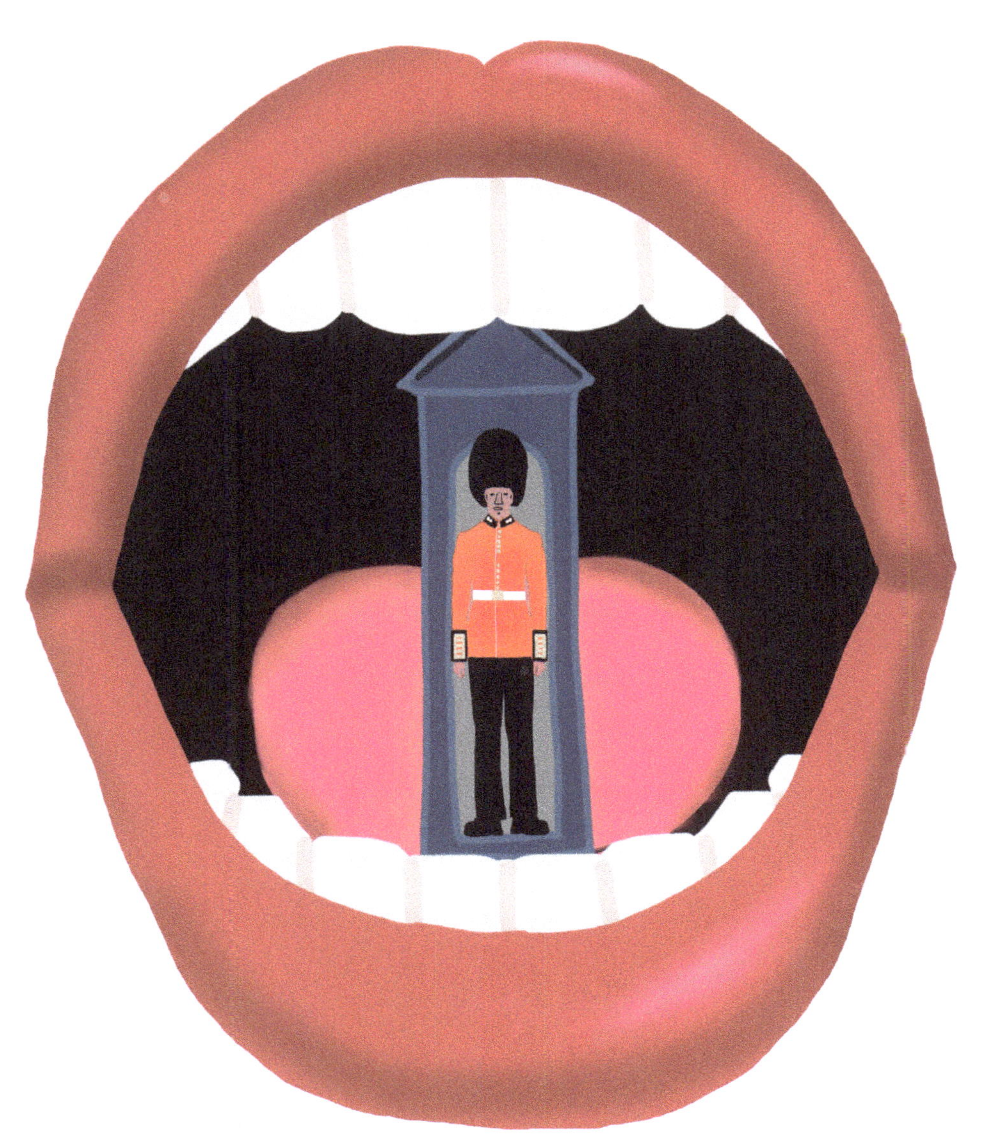

Mouth Guard

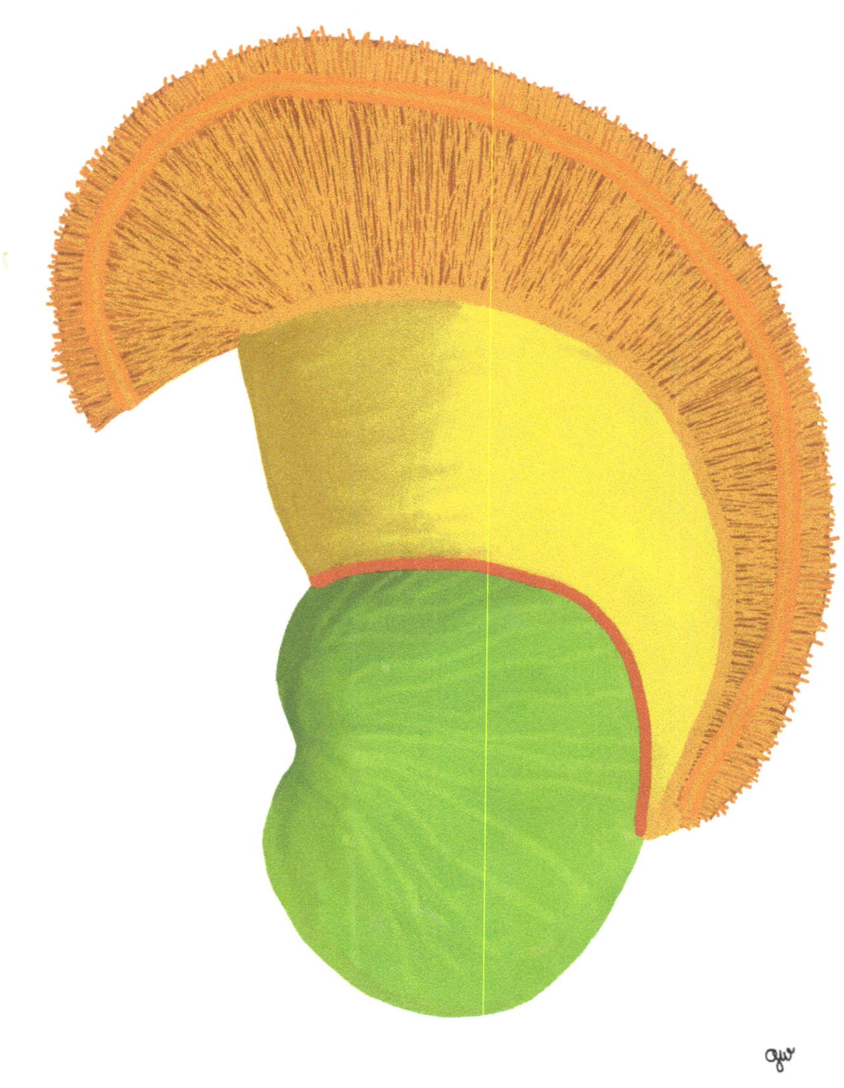

Dalai Lima

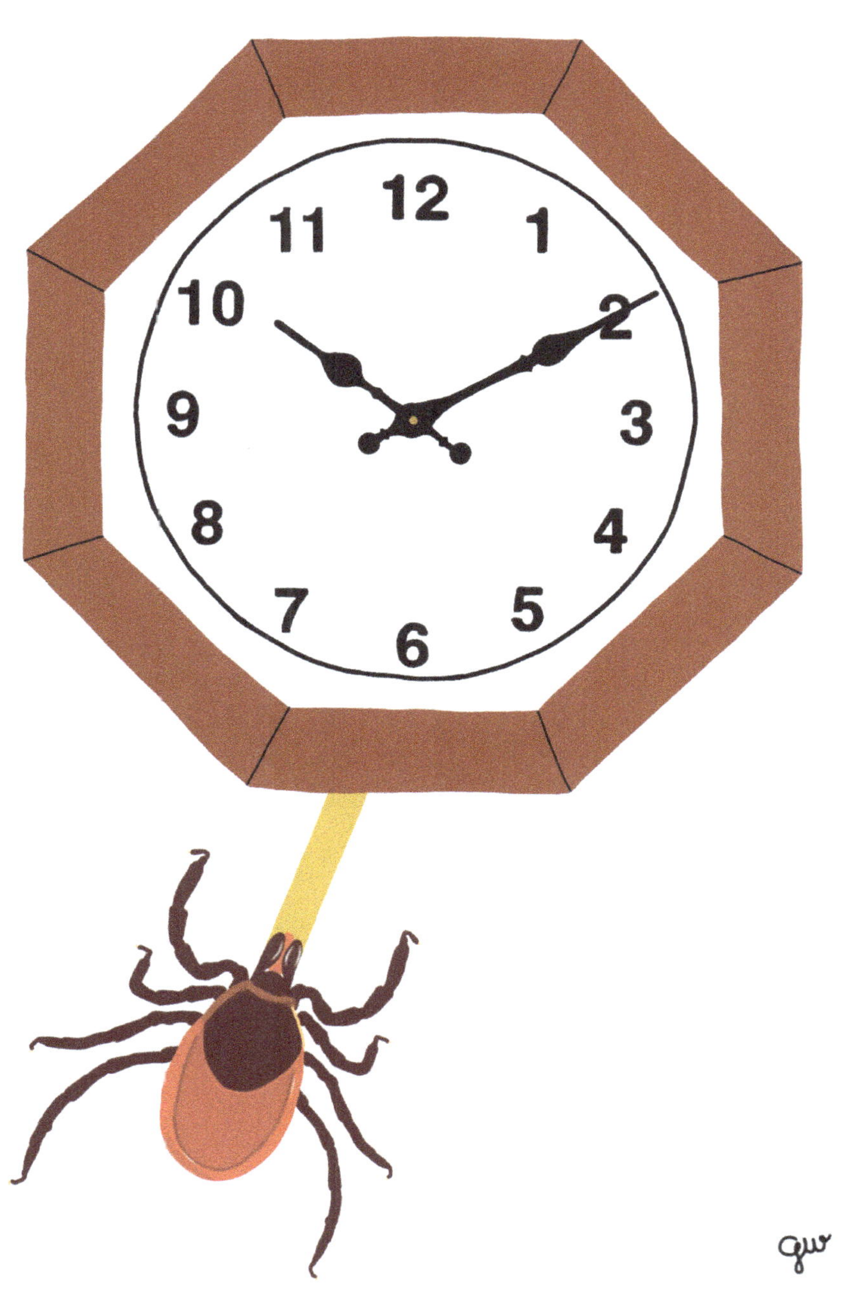

Tick Tock

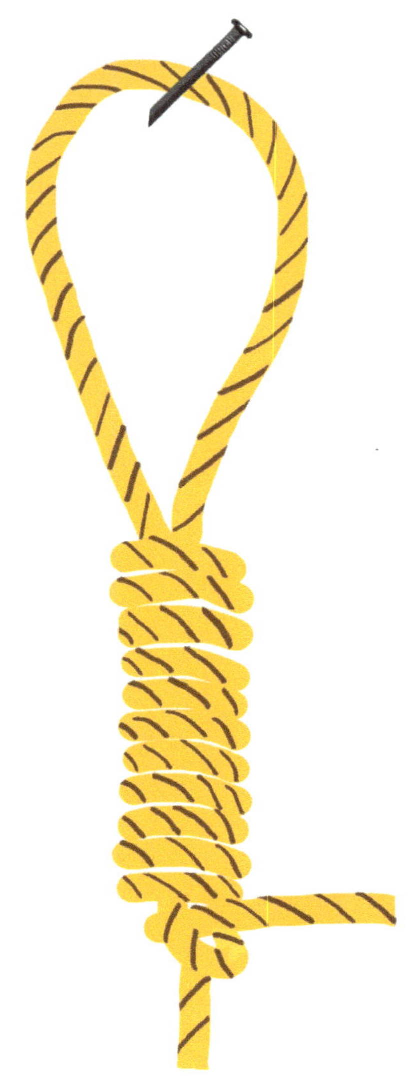

Hang Nail

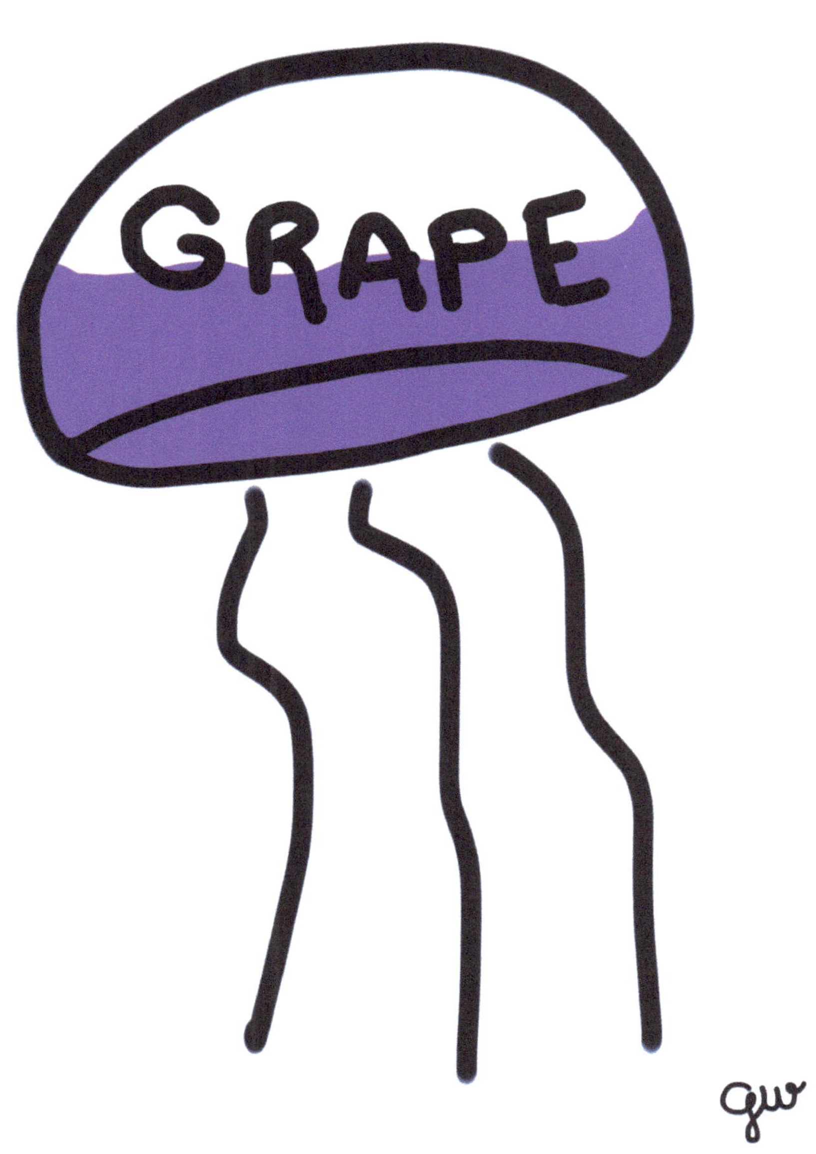

Jelly Fish

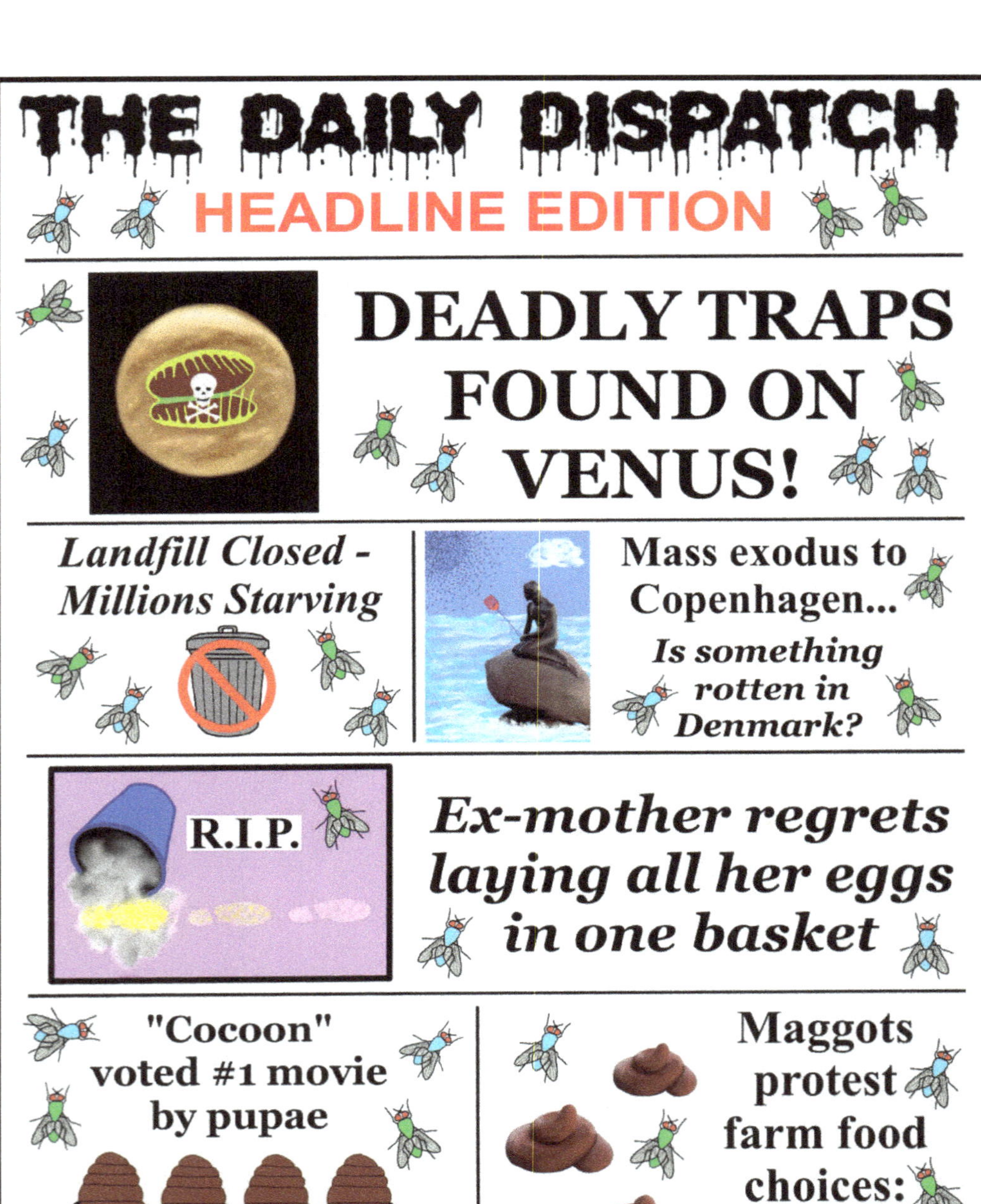
THE DAILY DISPATCH
HEADLINE EDITION
DEADLY TRAPS FOUND ON VENUS!
Landfill Closed - Millions Starving
Mass exodus to Copenhagen...
Is something rotten in Denmark?
R.I.P.
Ex-mother regrets laying all her eggs in one basket
"Cocoon" voted #1 movie by pupae
WE ♥ "COCOON"
Maggots protest farm food choices:
"We're sick of this crap!"

Fly Paper

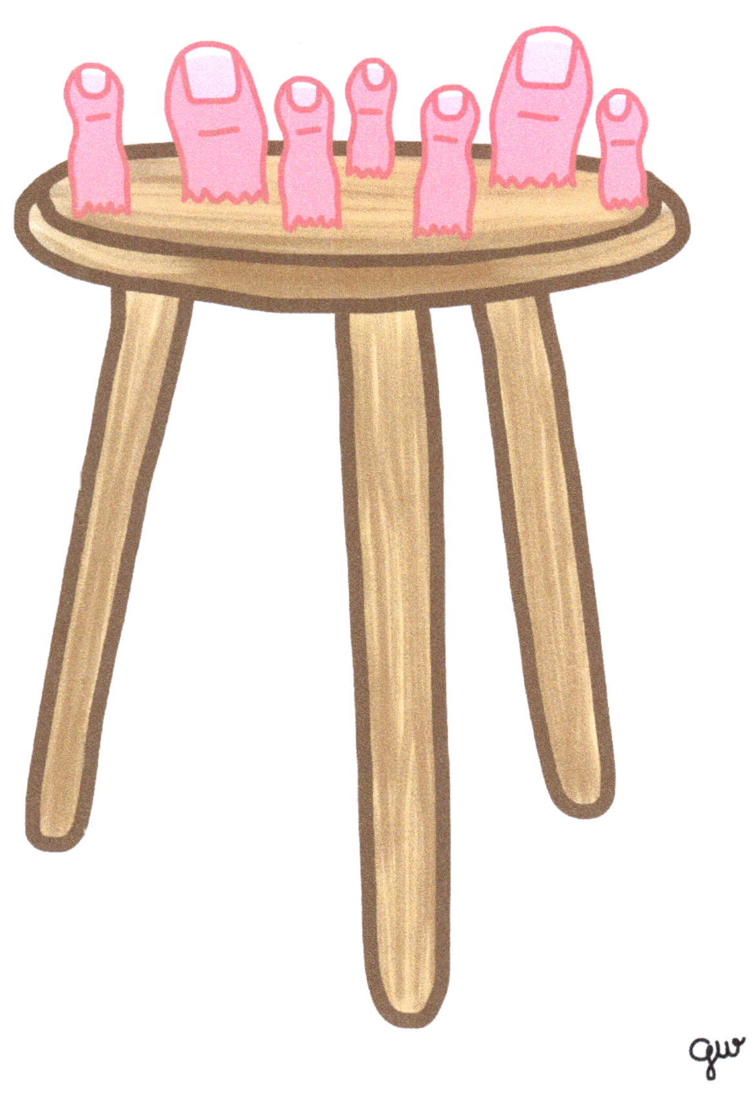

Toed Stool

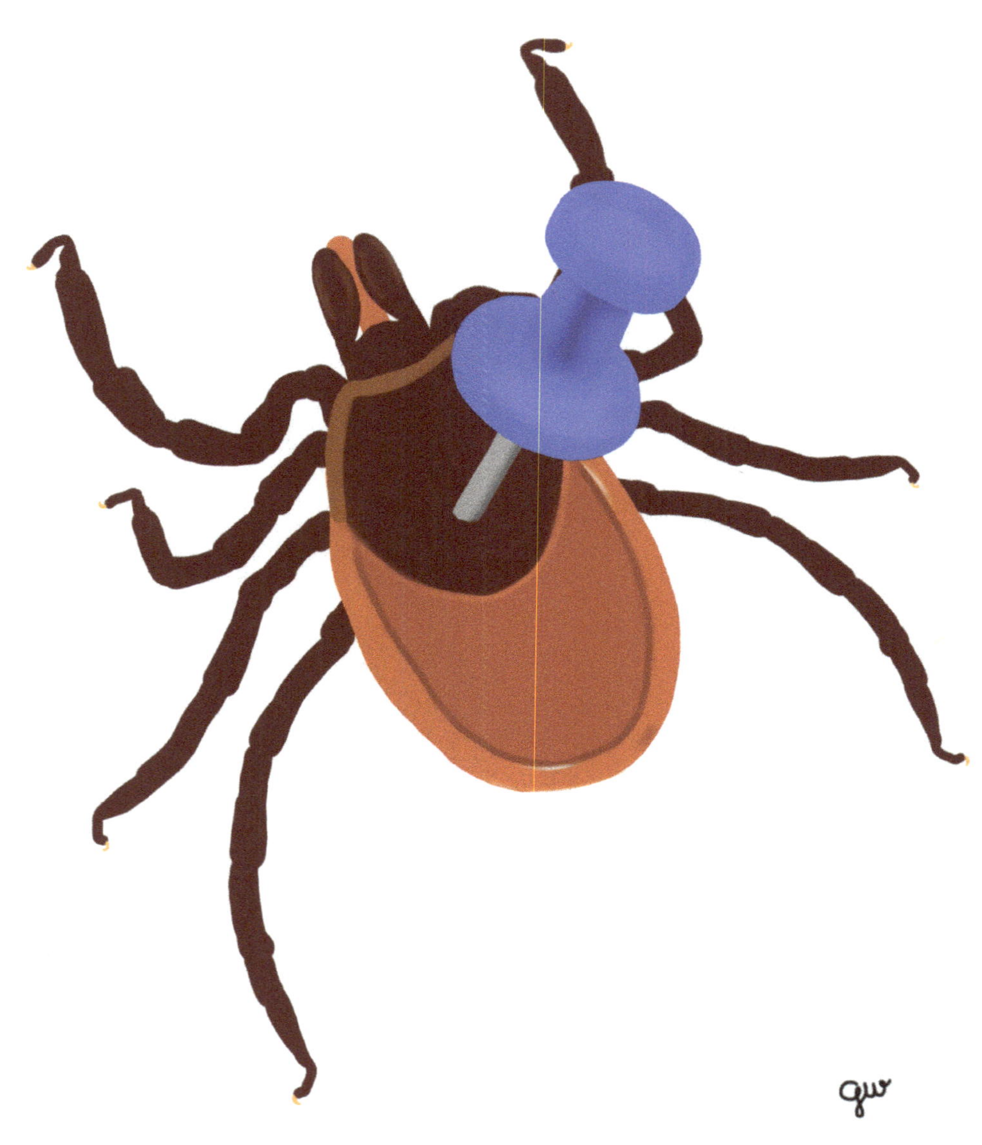

Tick Tack

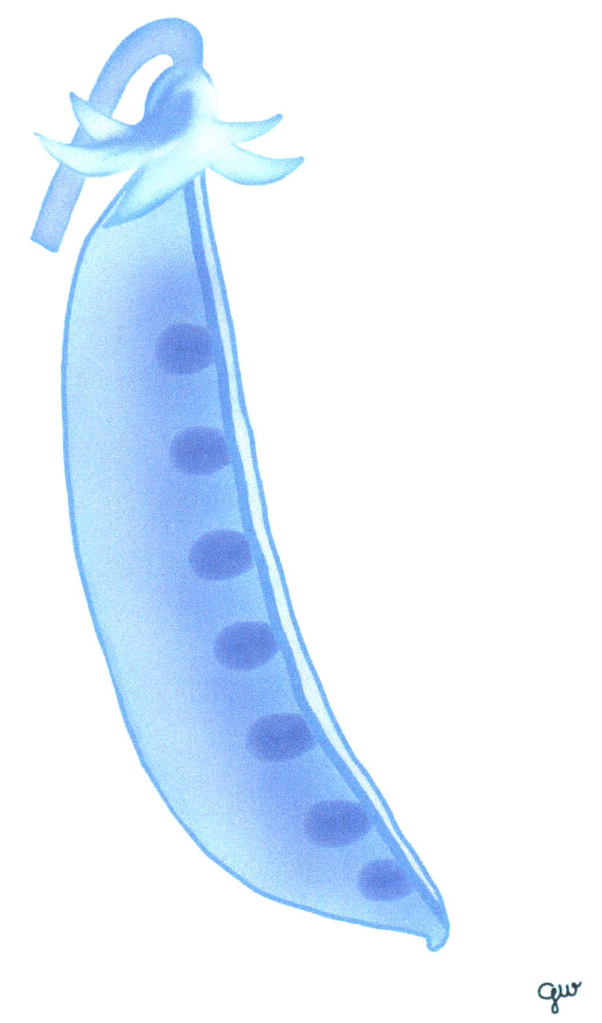

The Blue Legume

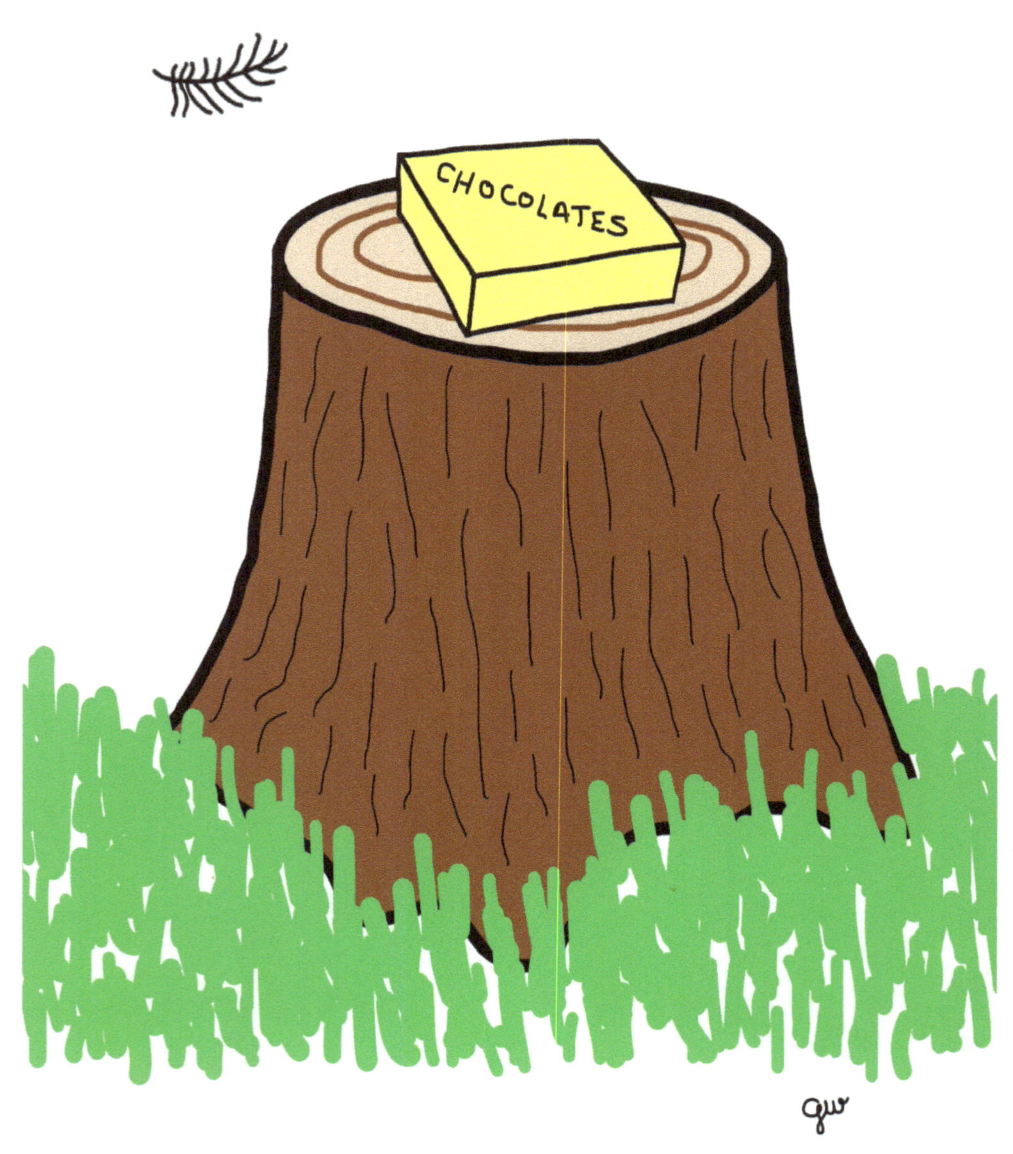

Forrest Stump

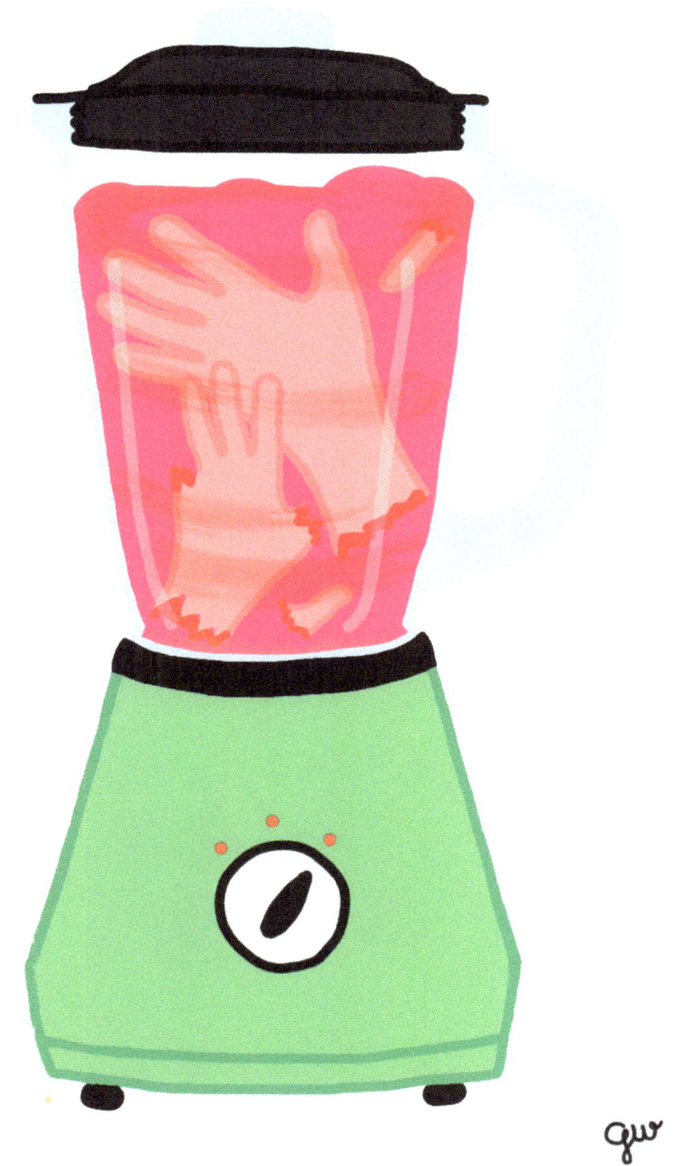

Hand Shake

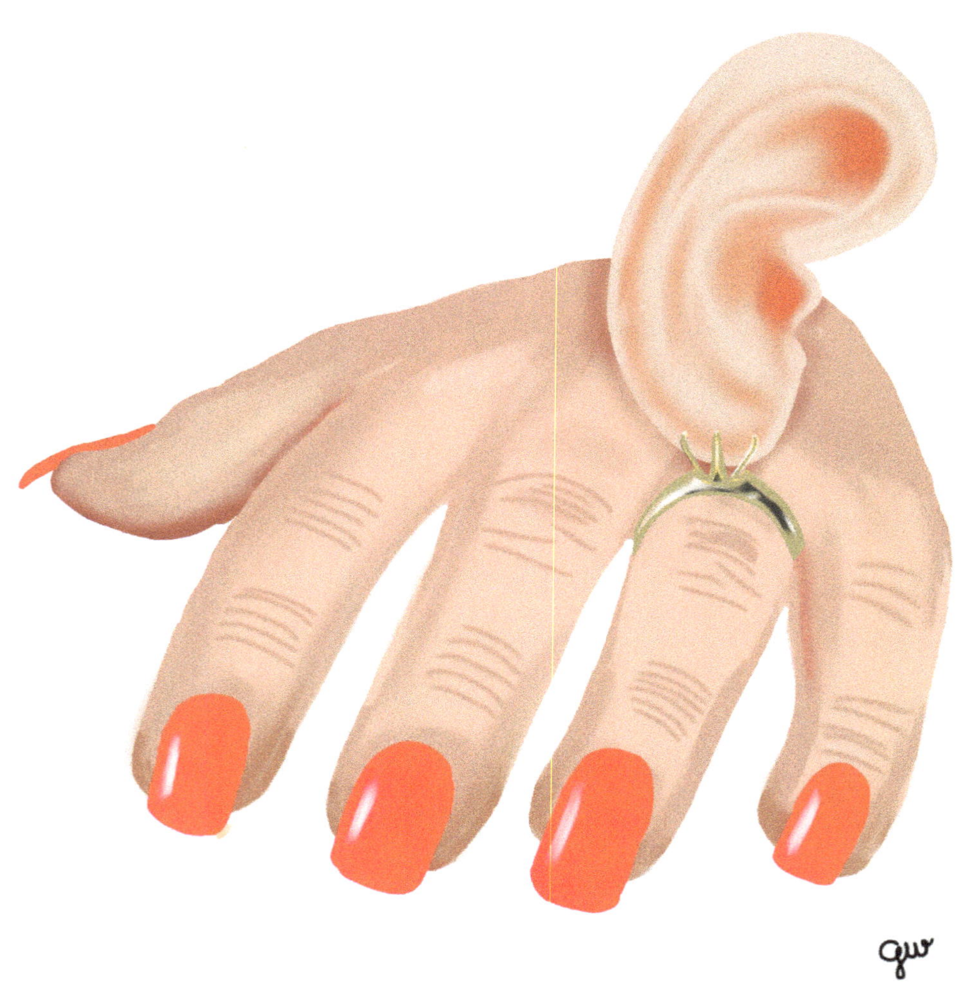

Ear Ring

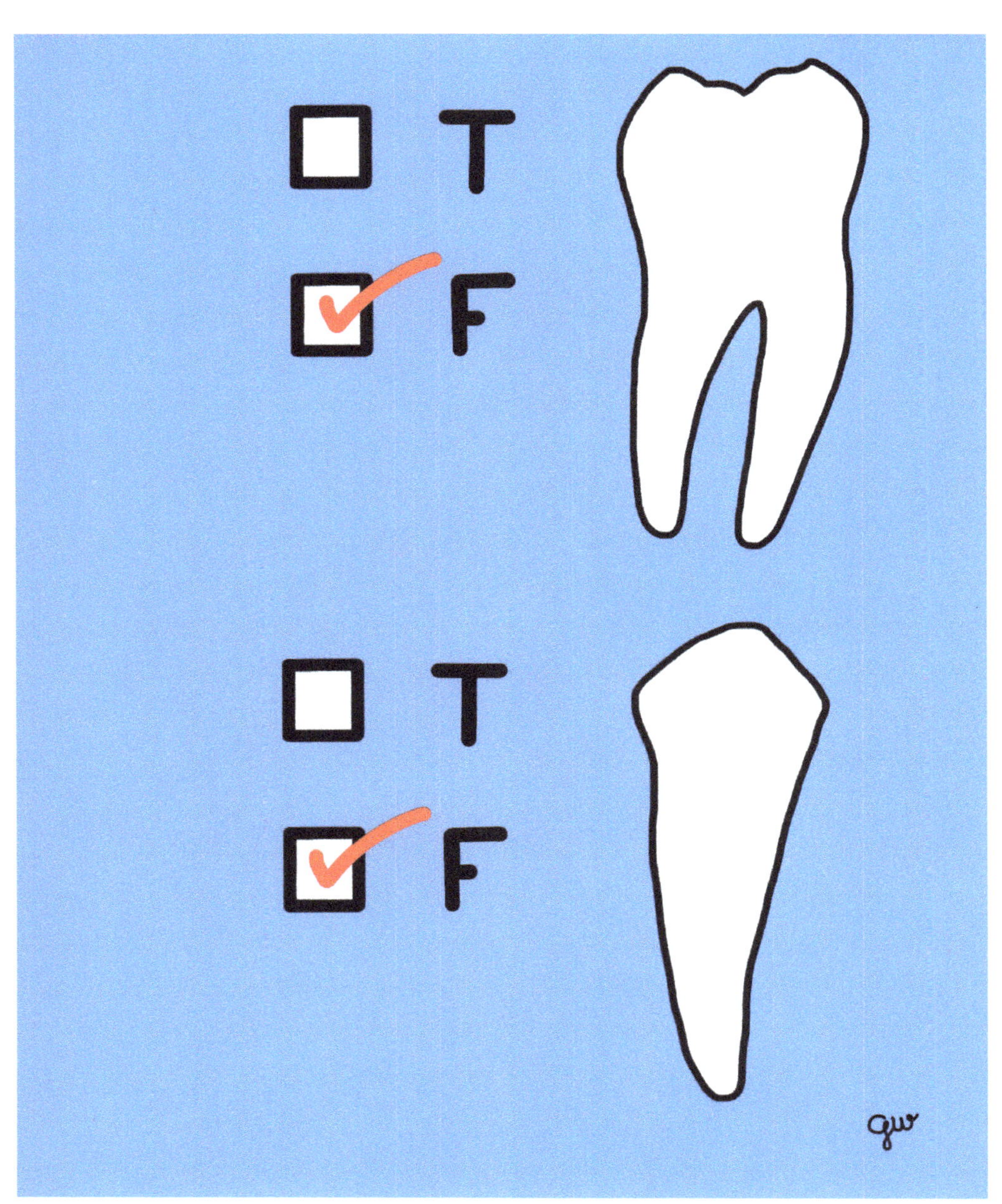

False Teeth

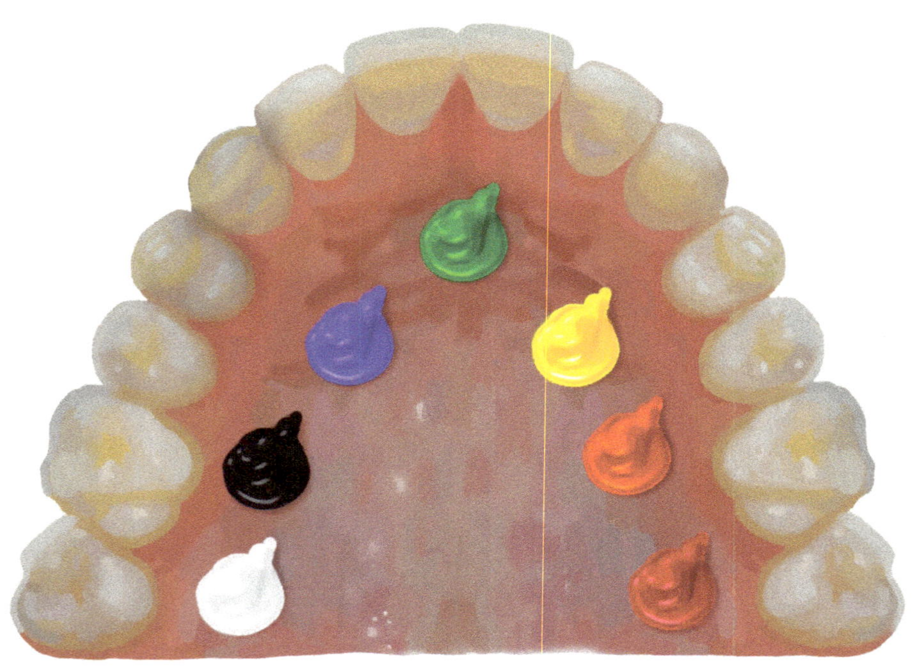

Artist's Palate

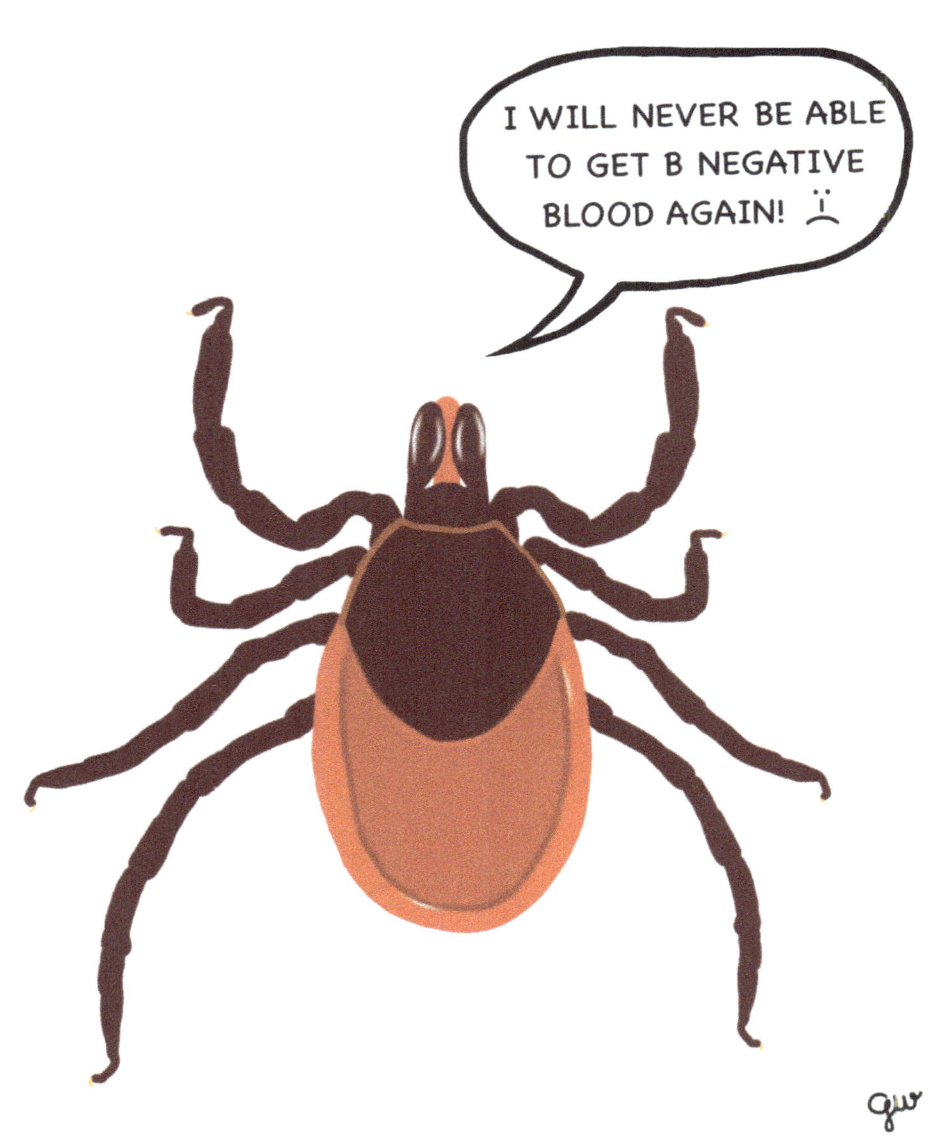

Pessimist Tick

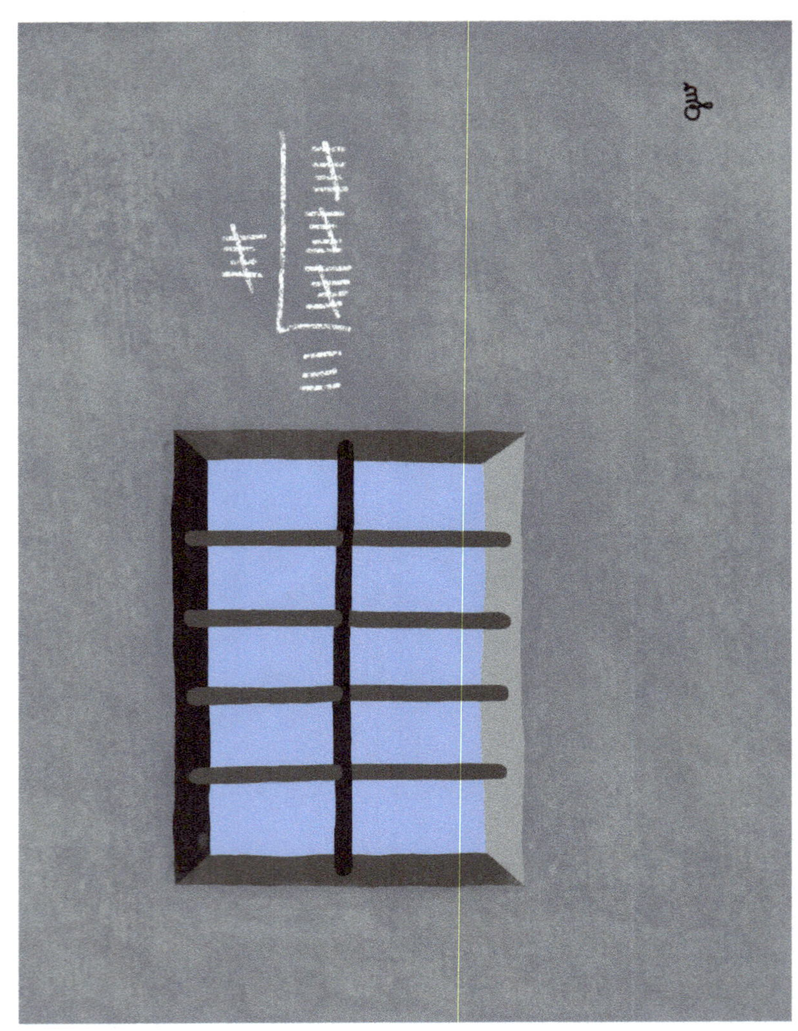

Cell Division

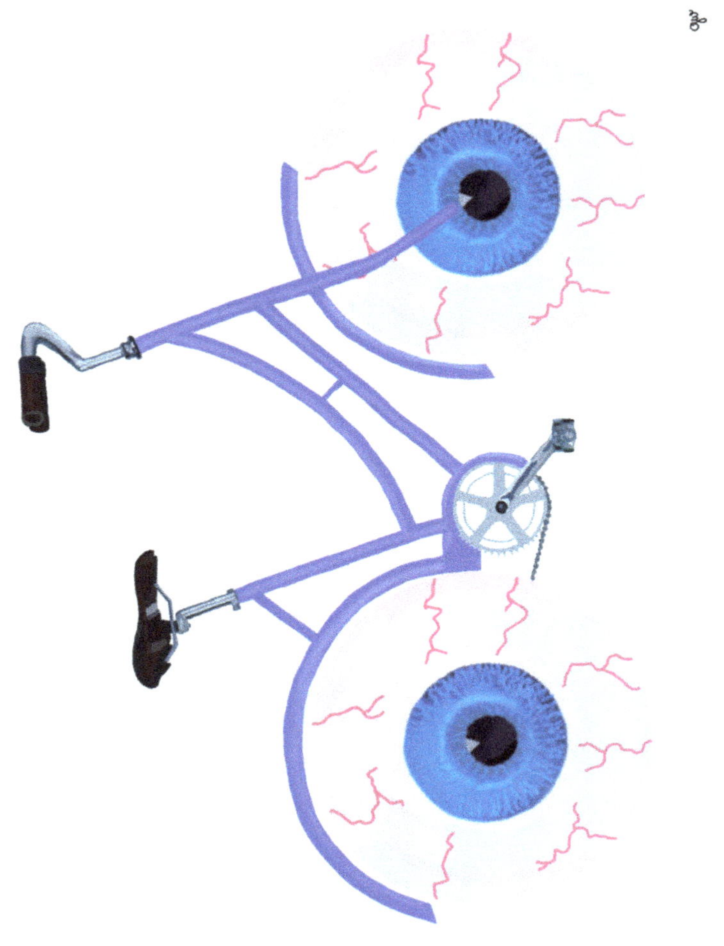

Eyecycle

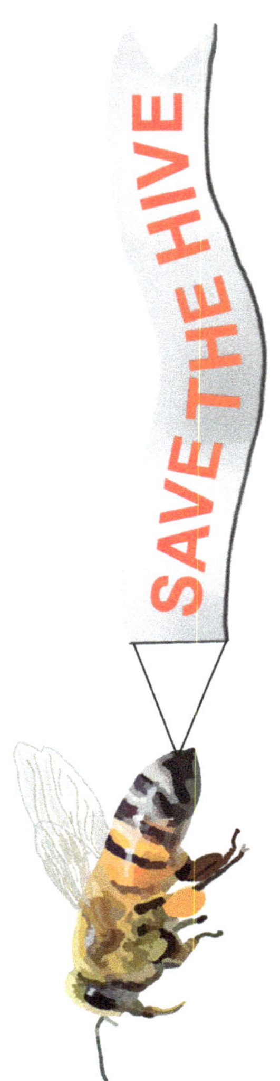

Bee Cause

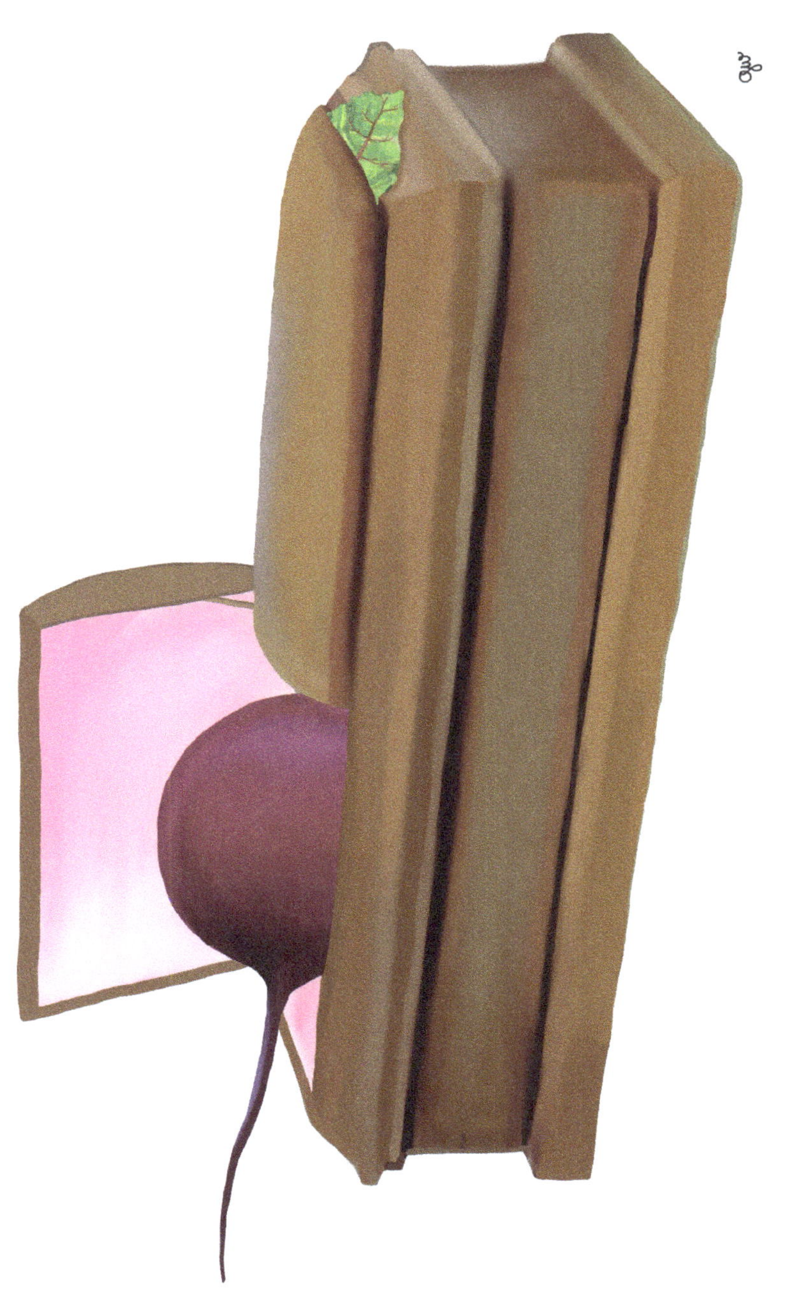

Dead Beet

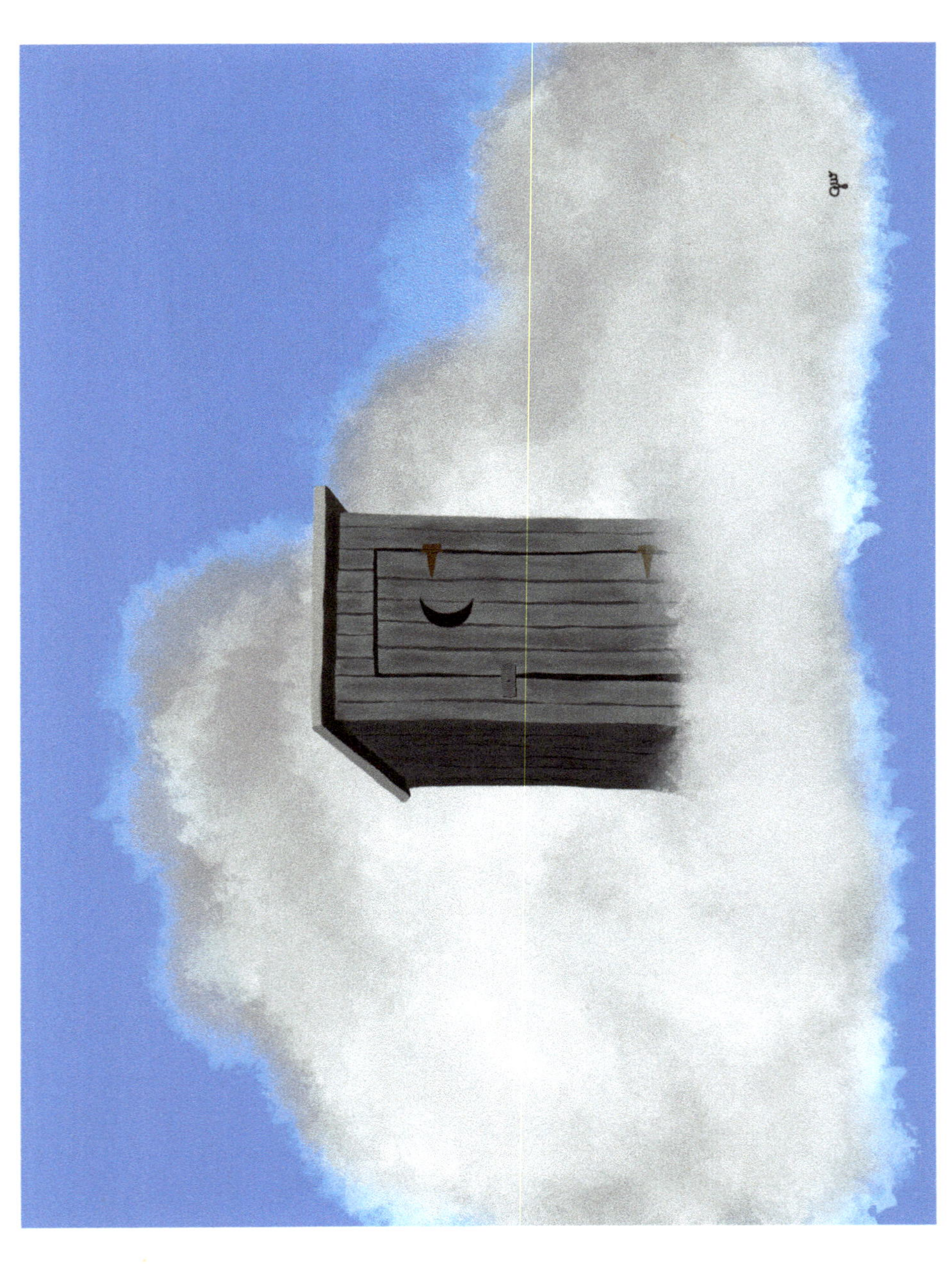

Head in the Clouds

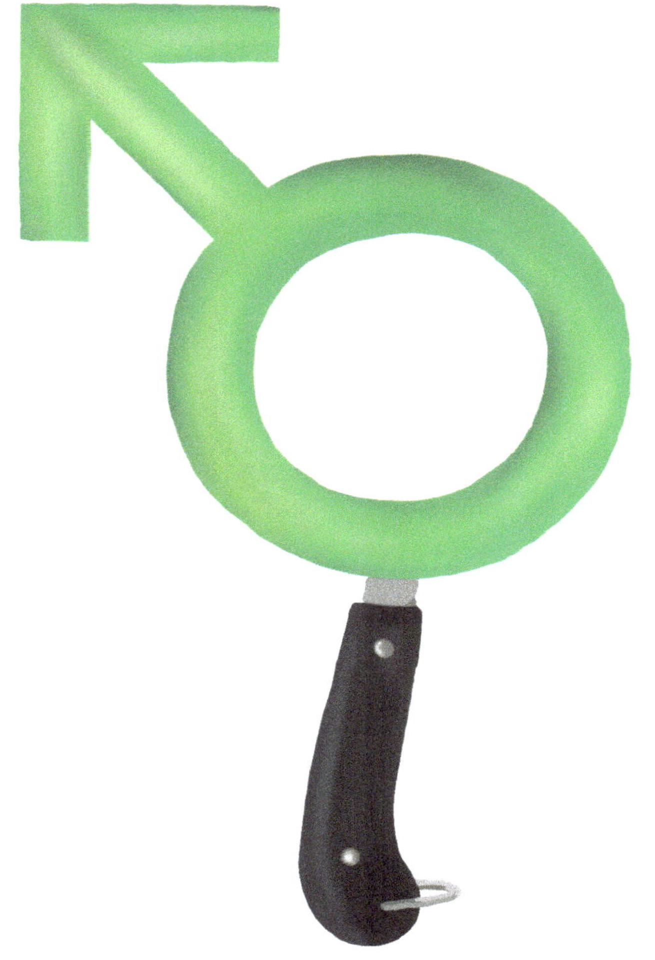

Man Handle

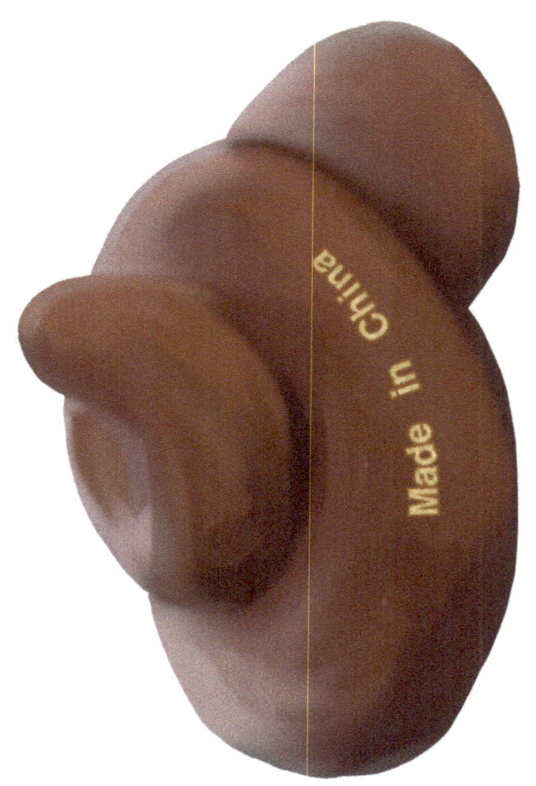

Sham Poo

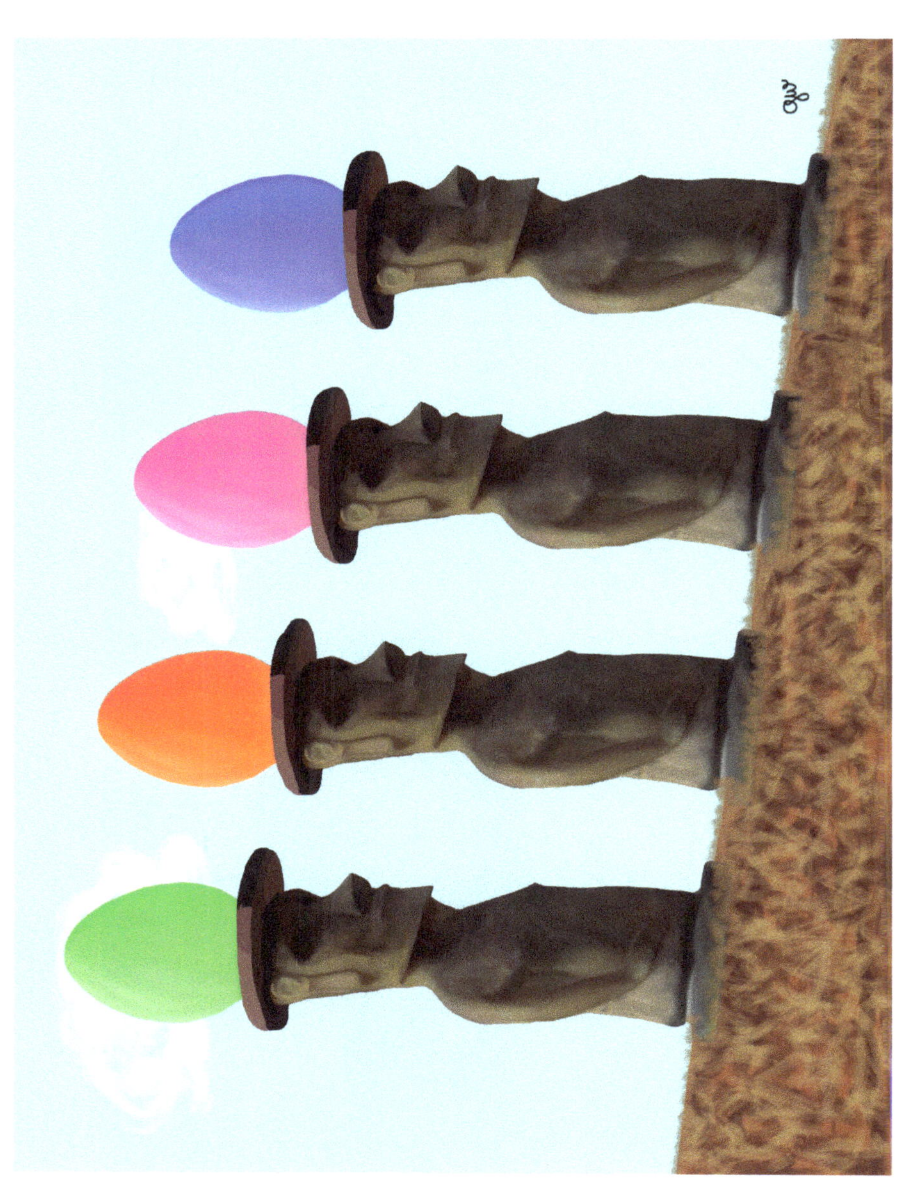

Easter Island

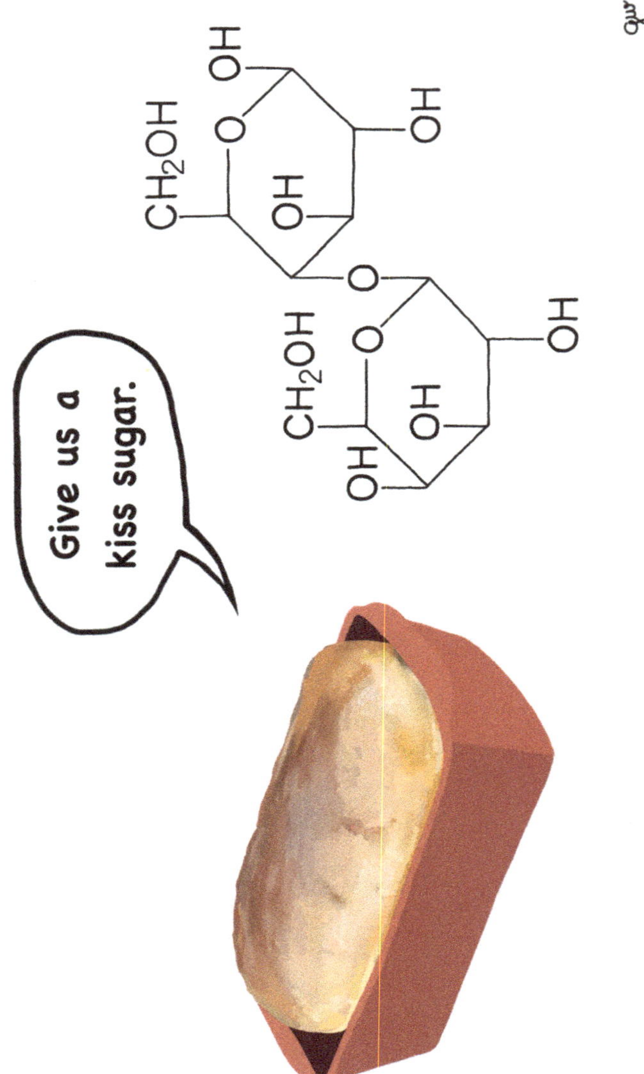

Fresh Bread

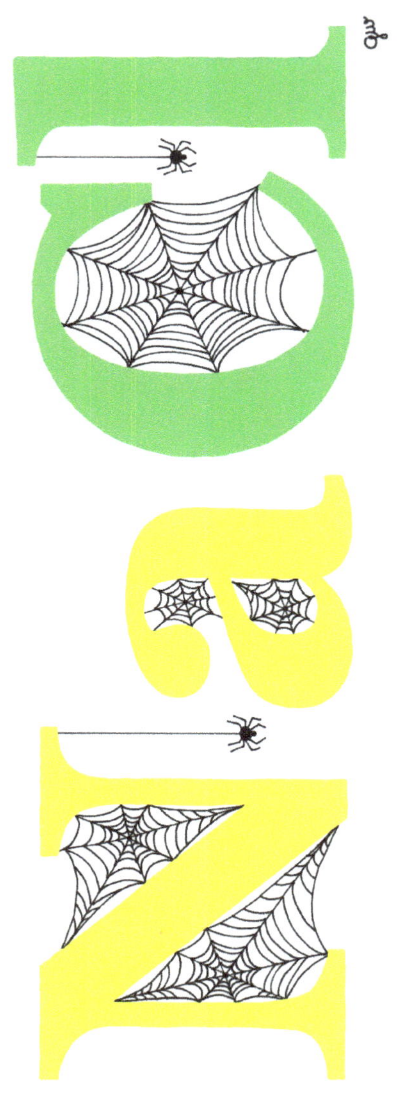

Old Salt

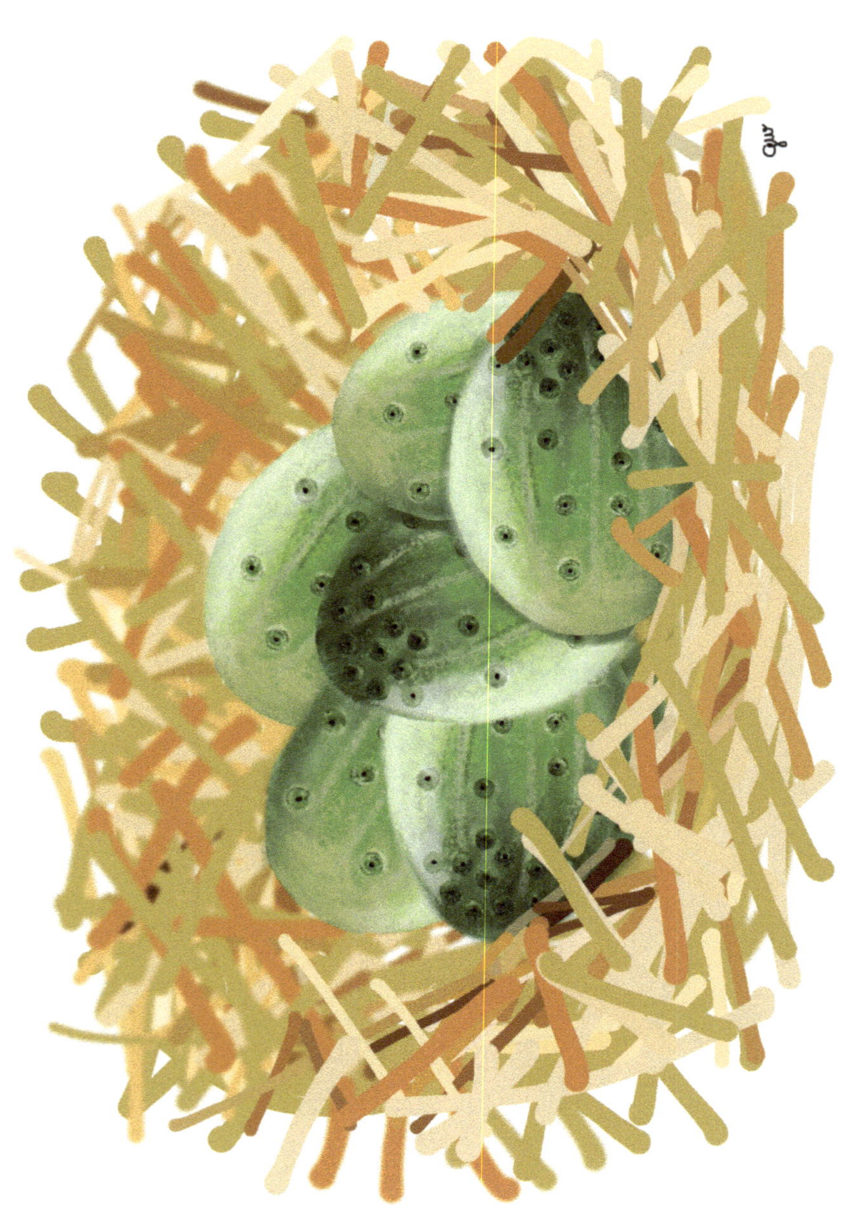

Pickled Eggs

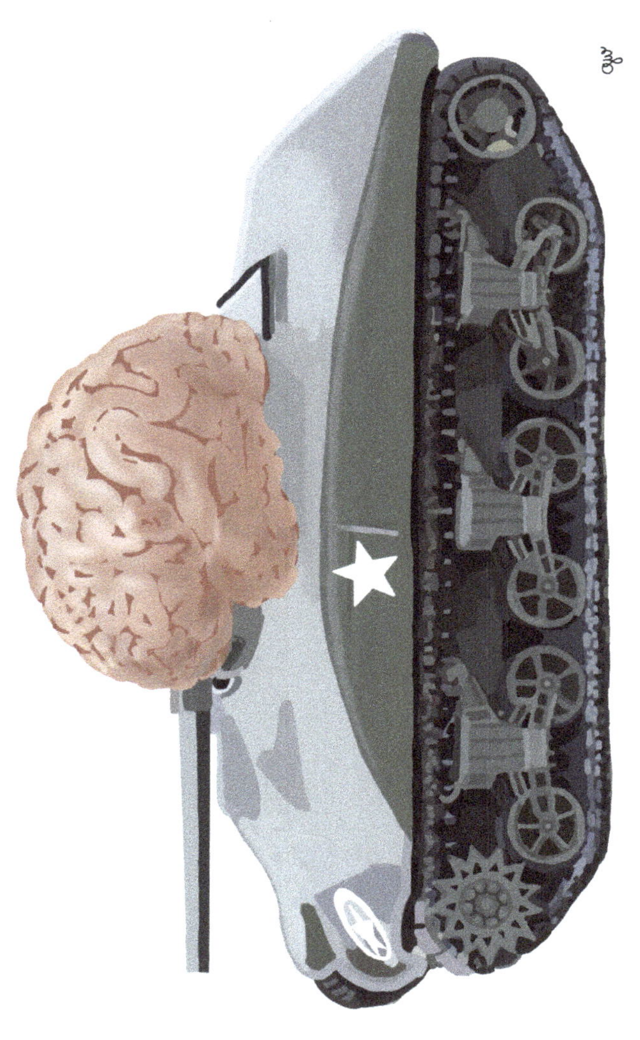

Think Tank

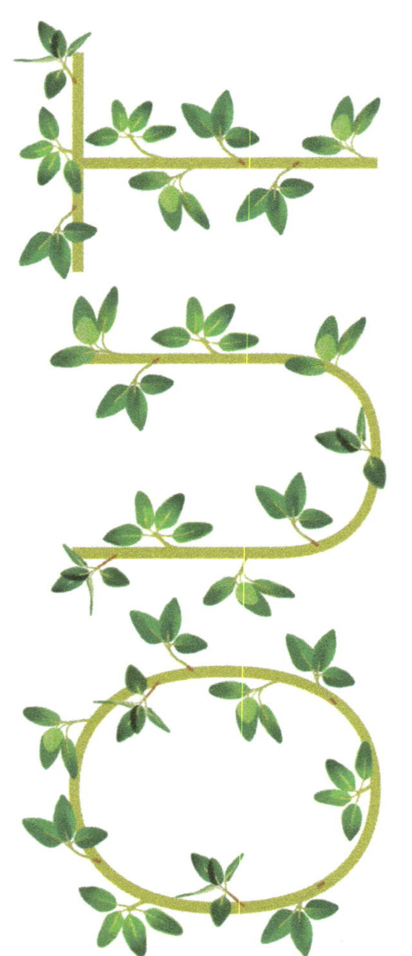

Thyme Out

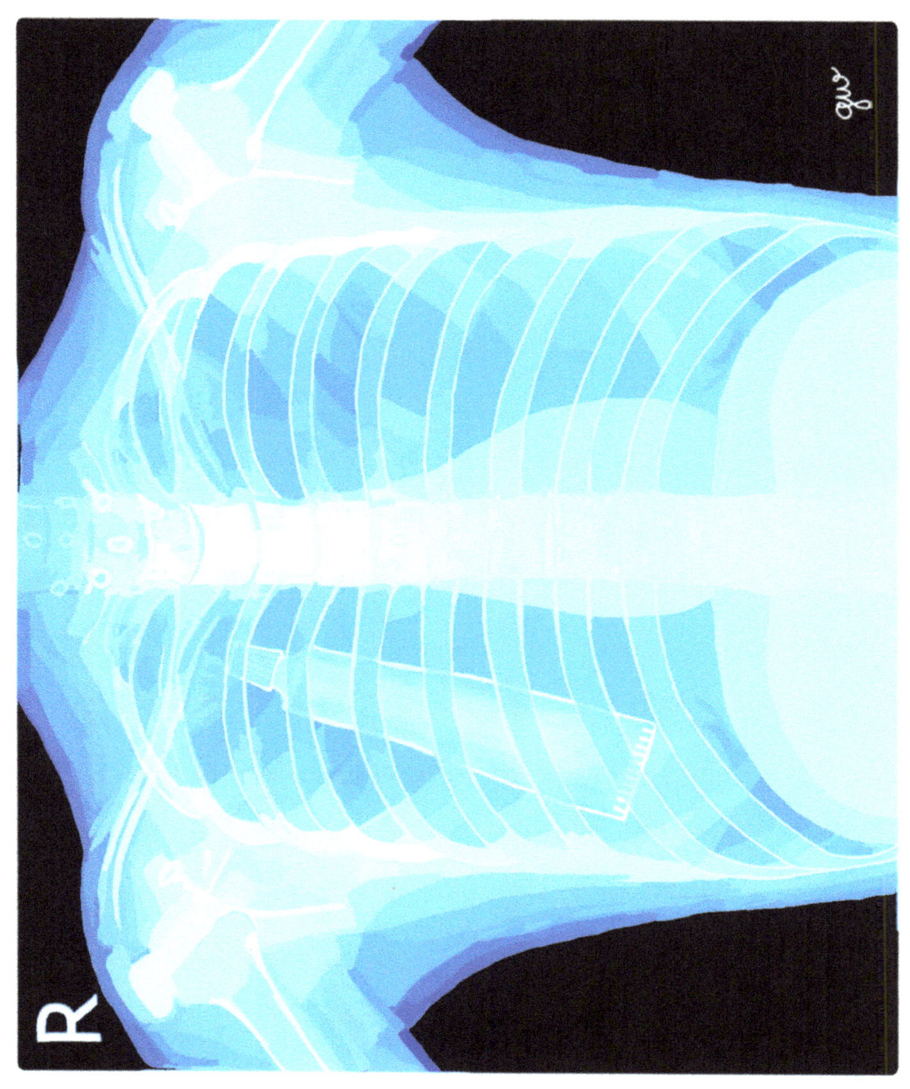

Inner Tube

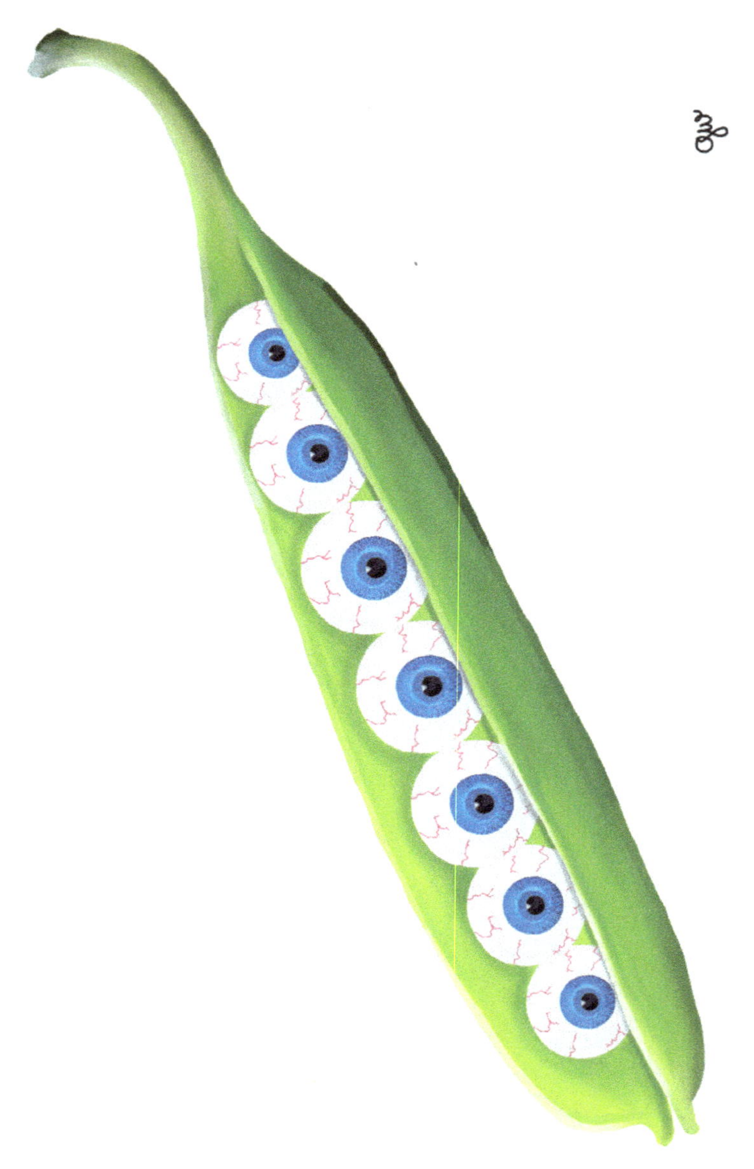

Eye Pod

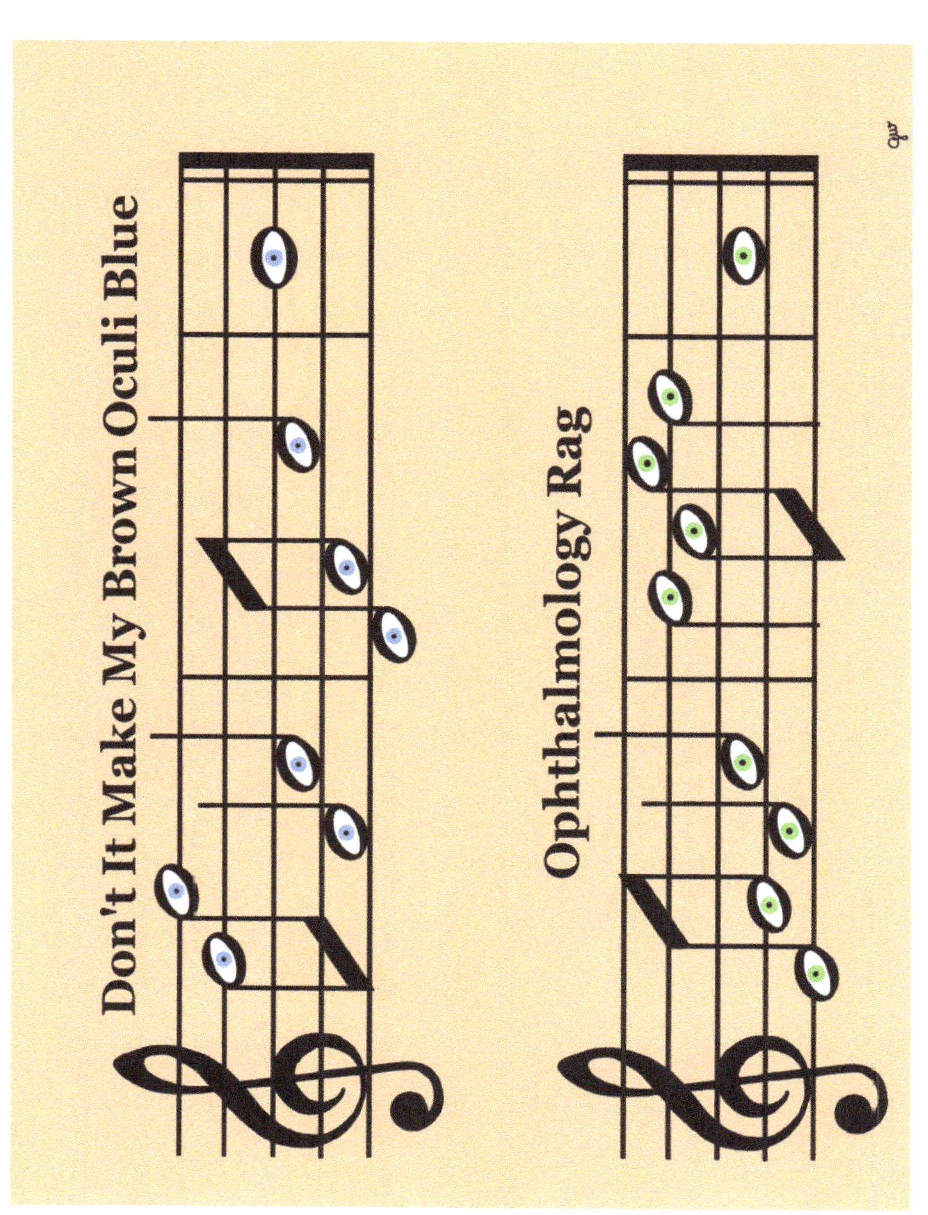

Eye Tunes

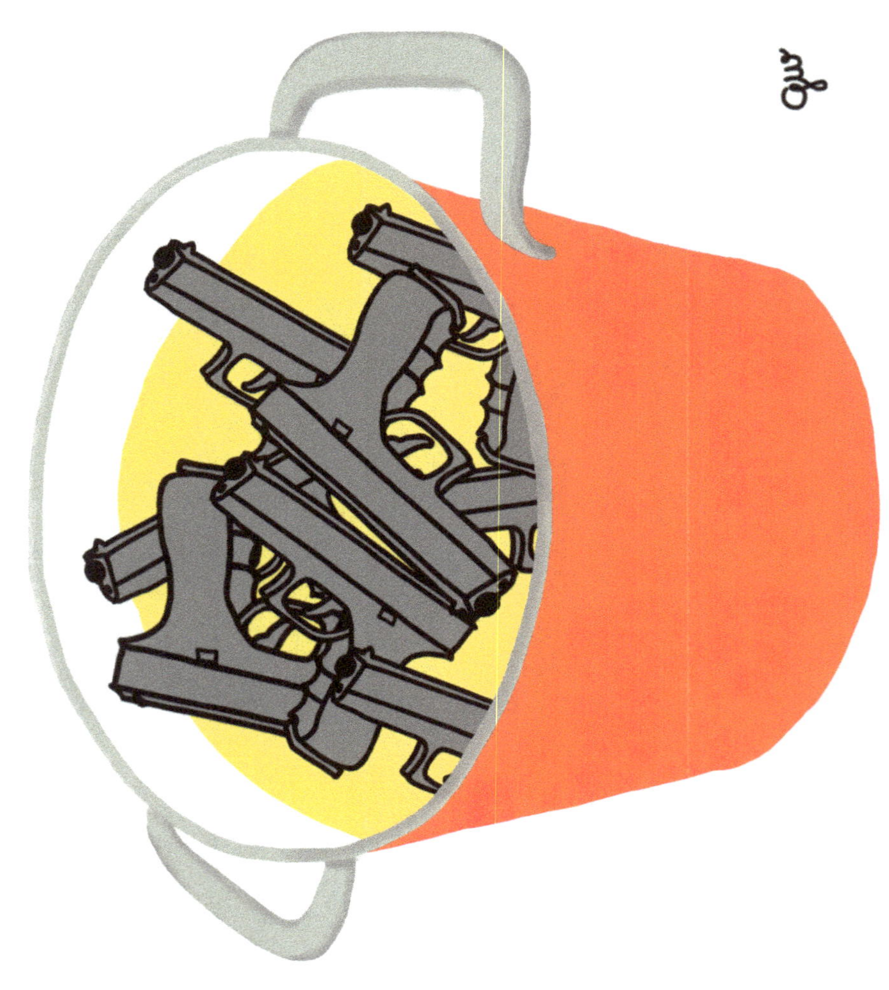

Too Many Crooks
Spoil The Broth

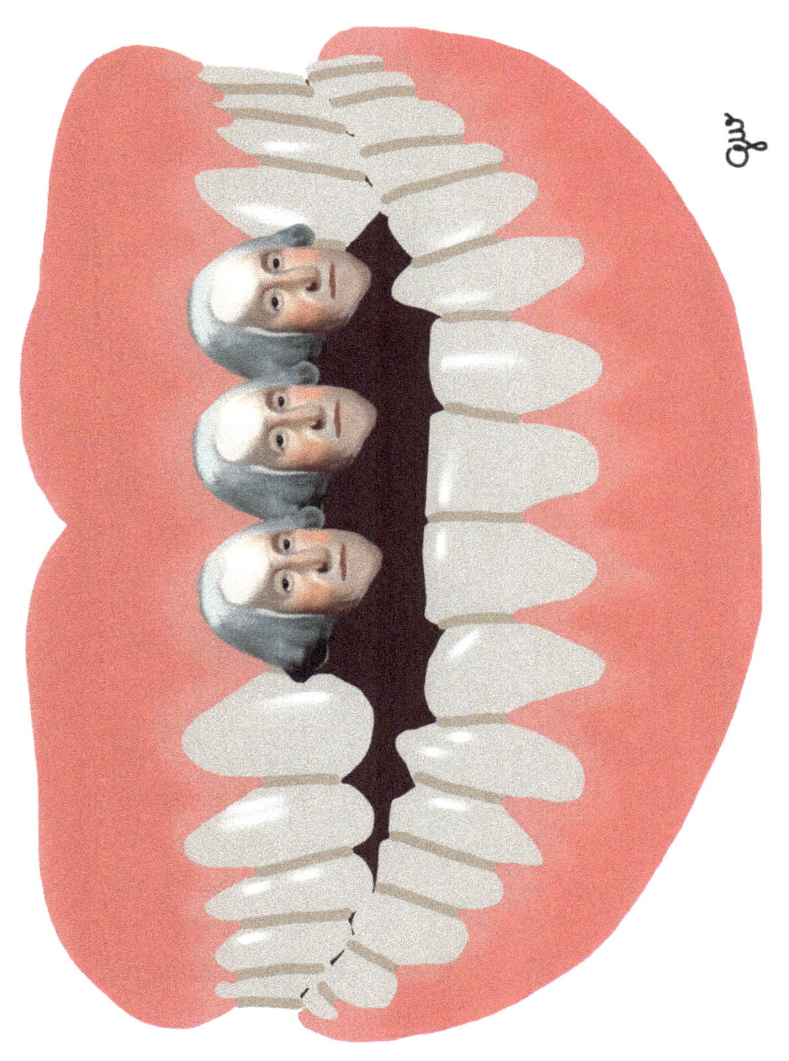

George Washington Bridge

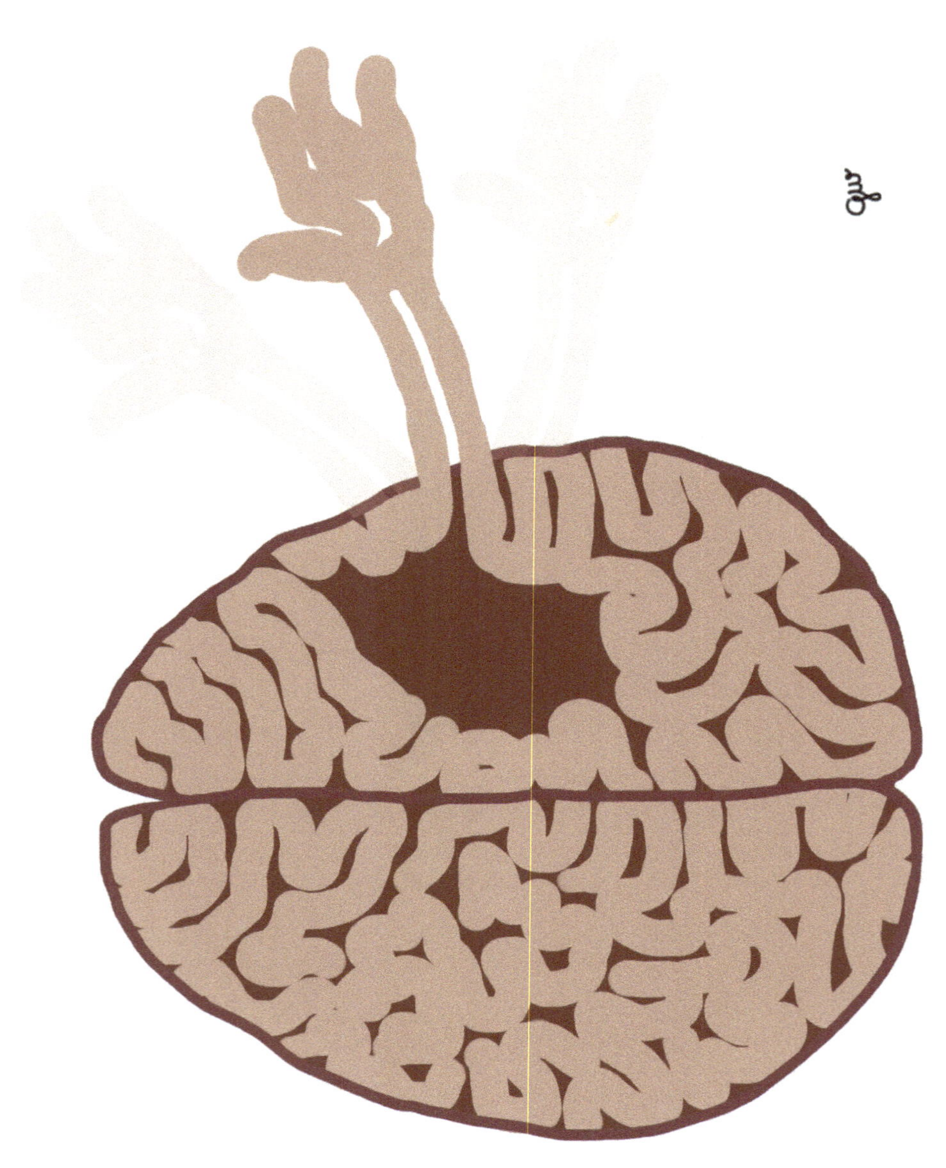

Brain Wave

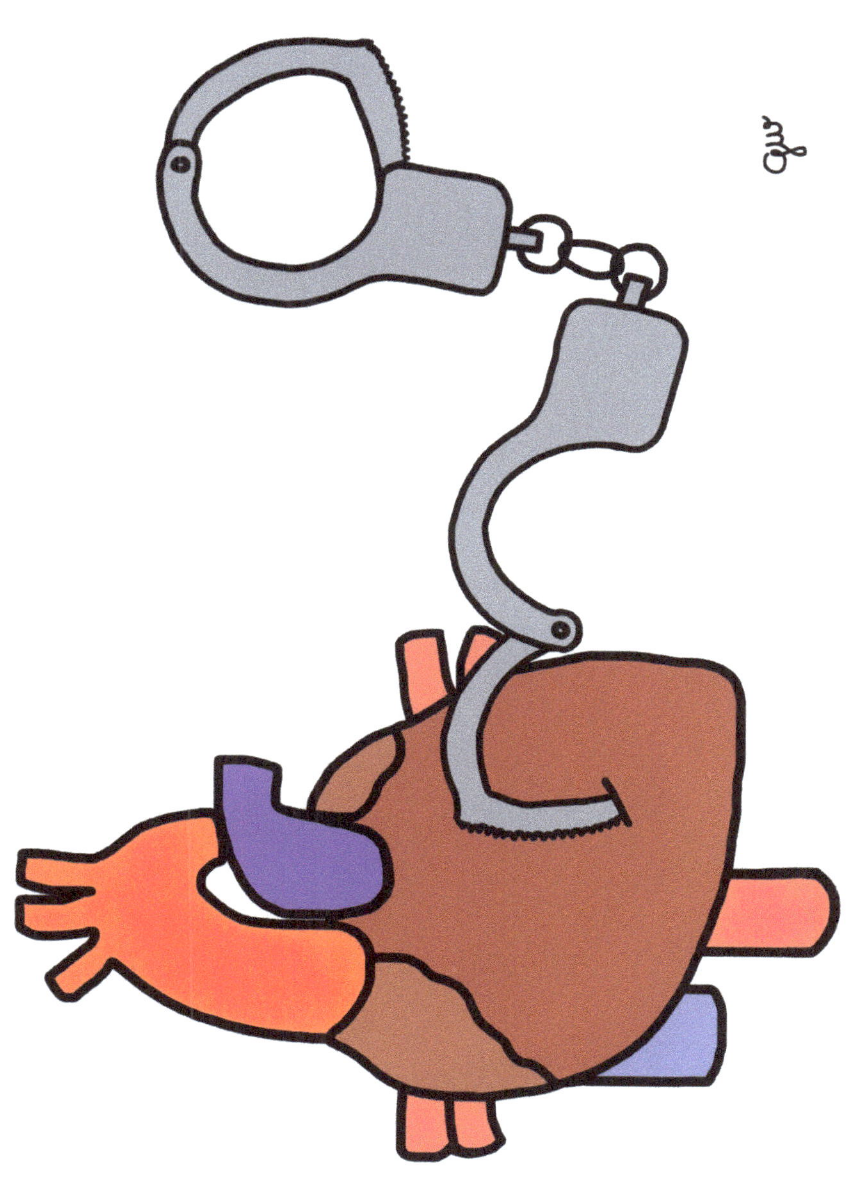

Cardiac Arrest

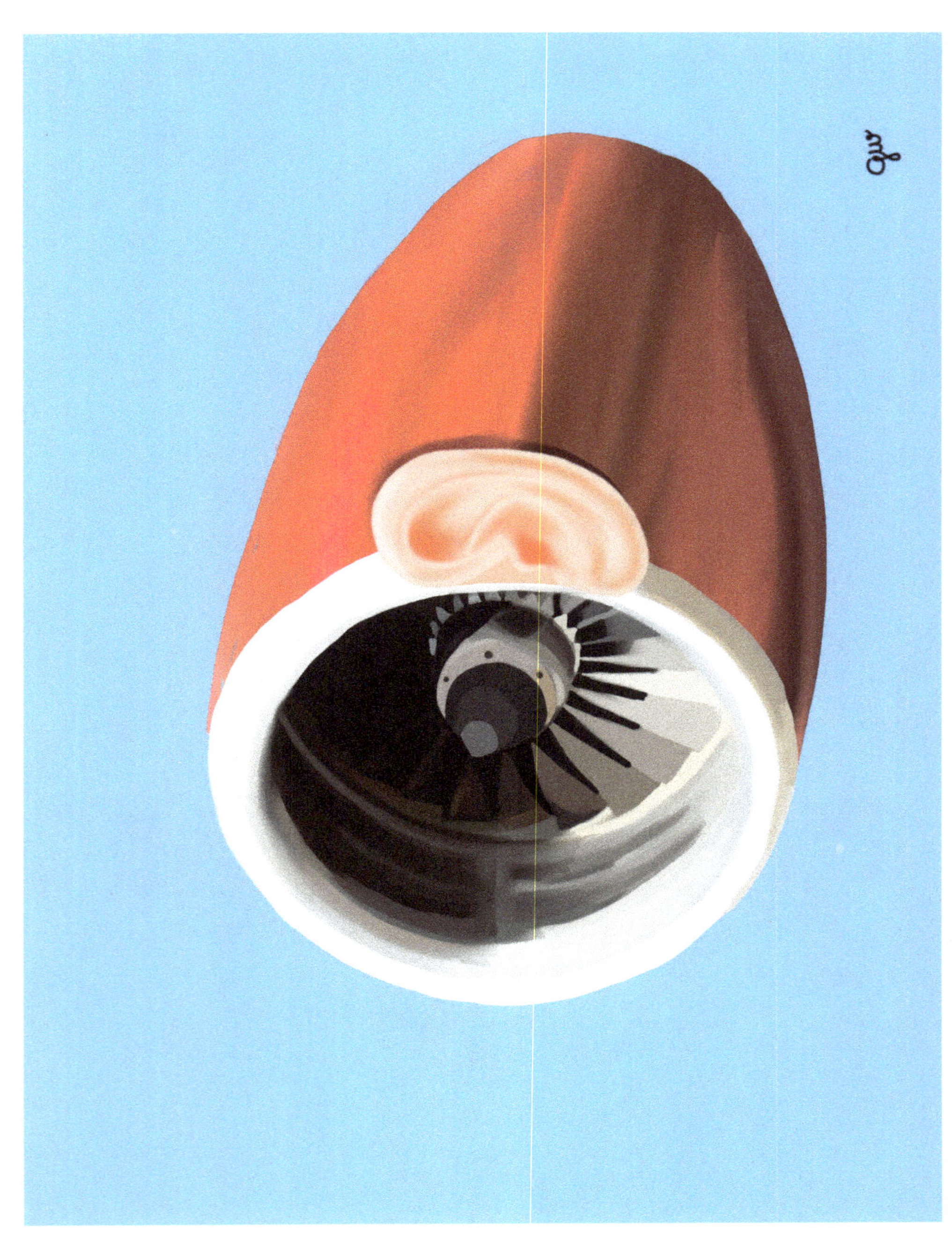

Engine Ear

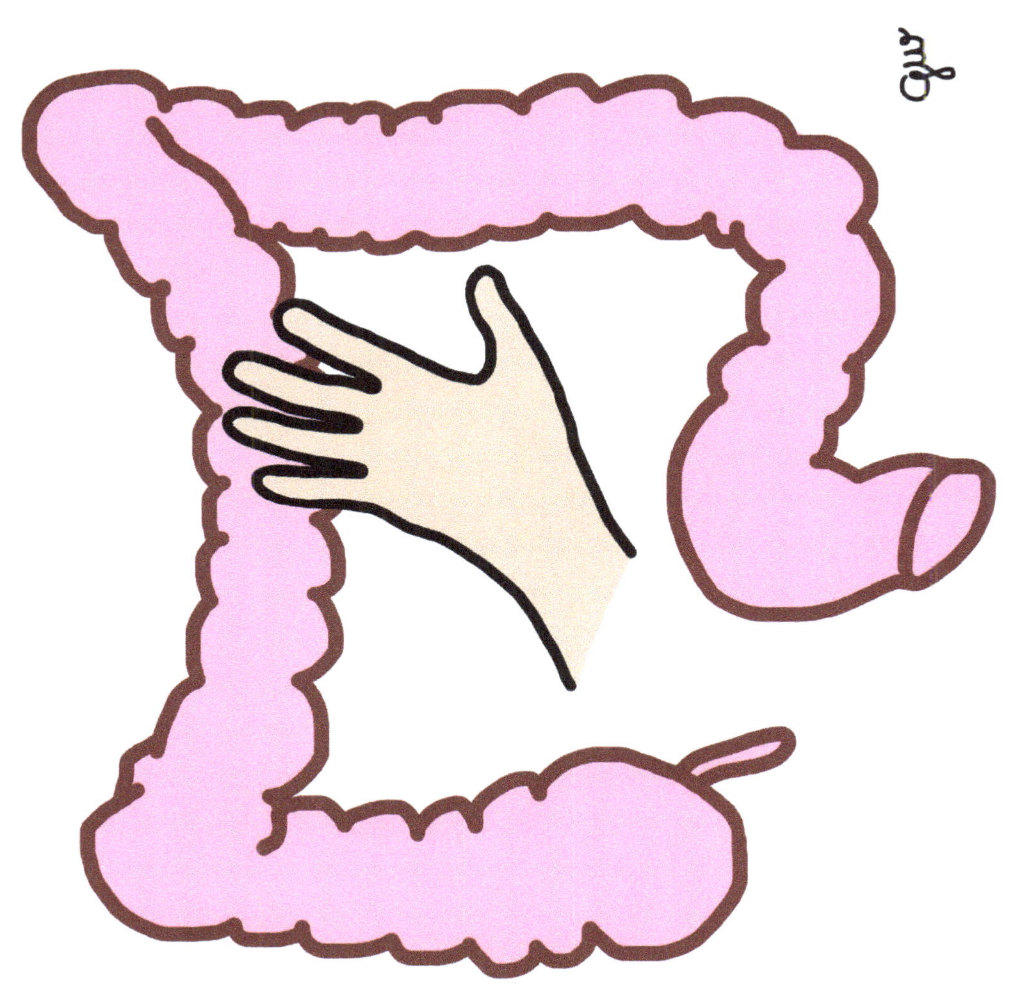

Gut Feeling

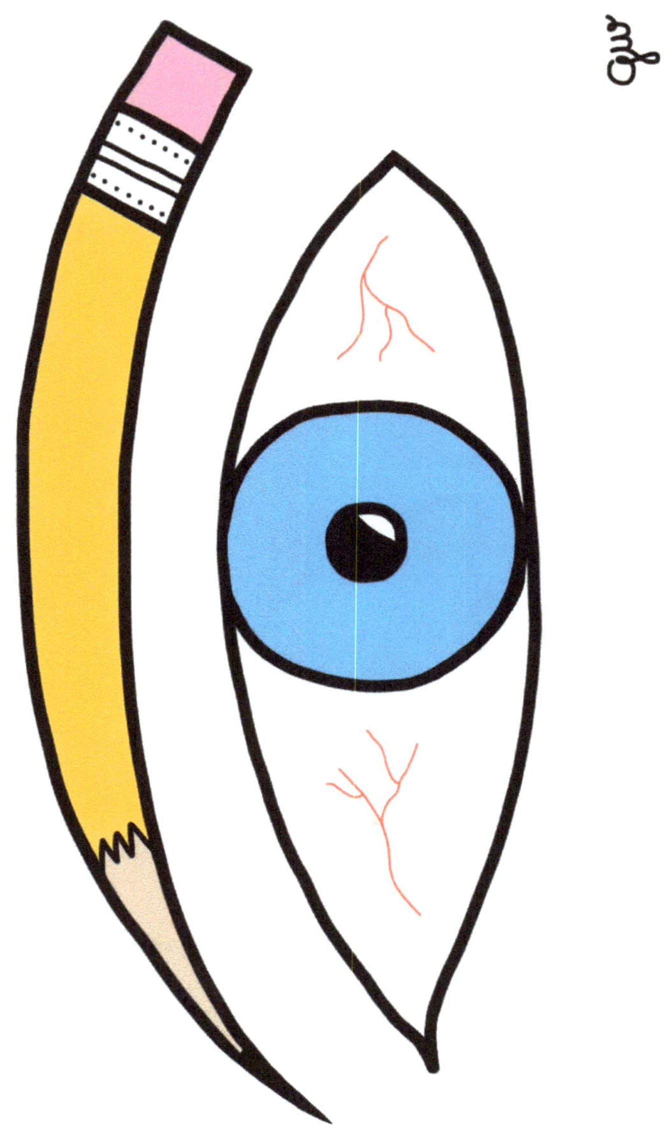

Eyebrow Pencil

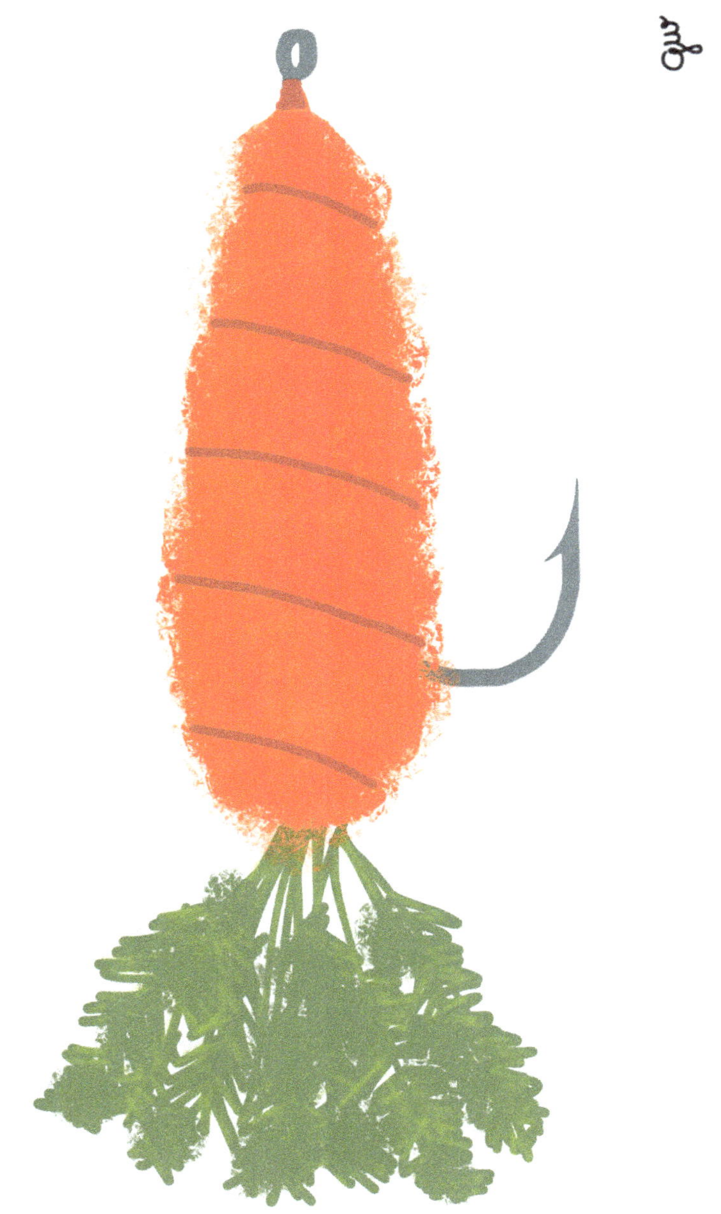

Horse Fly

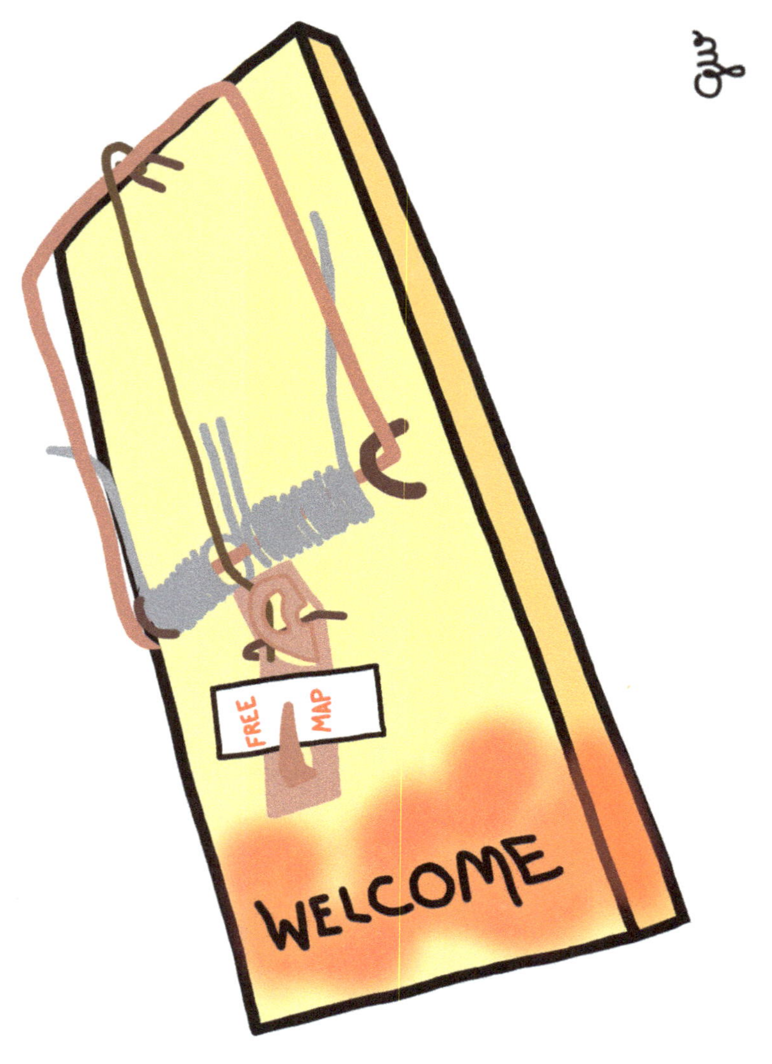

Tourist Trap

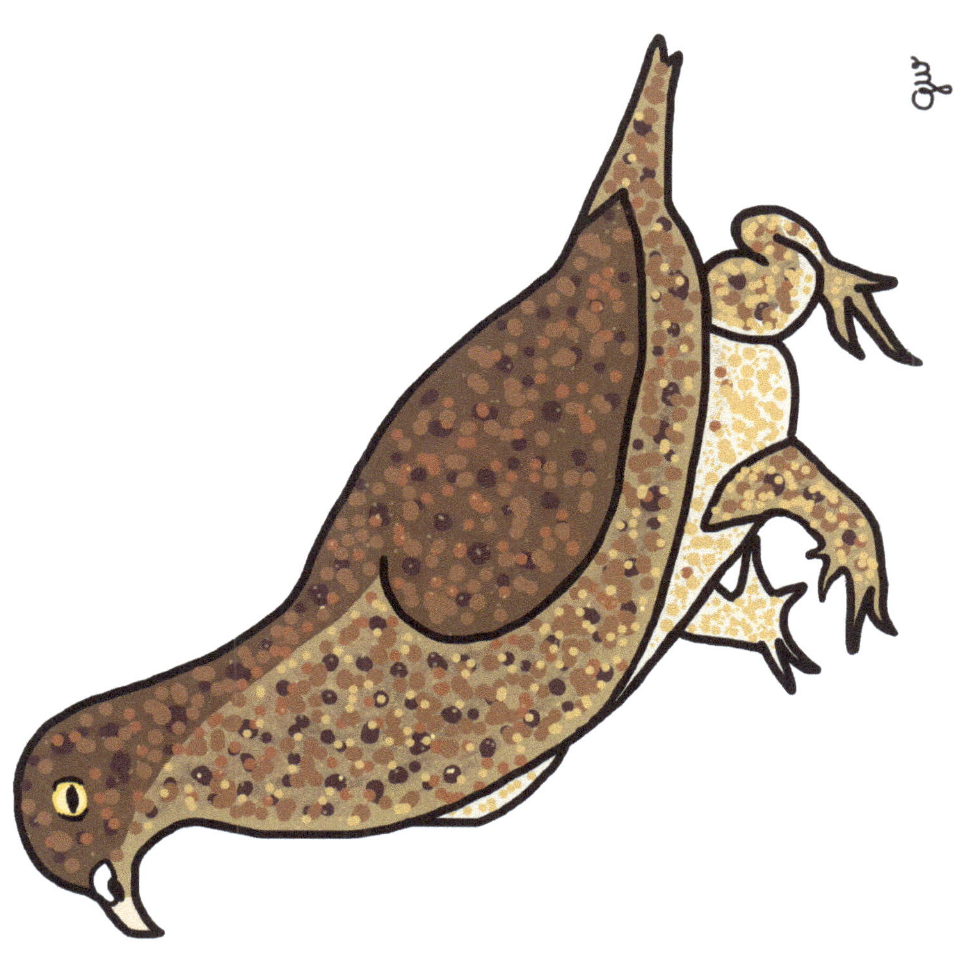

Pigeon Toad

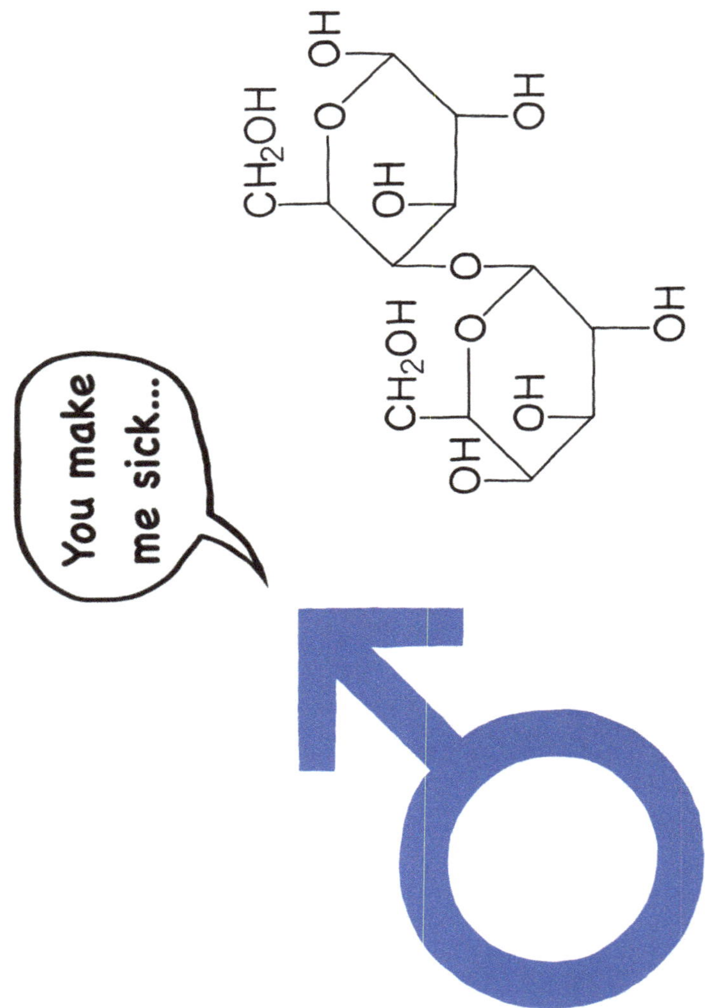

Lactose Intolerance

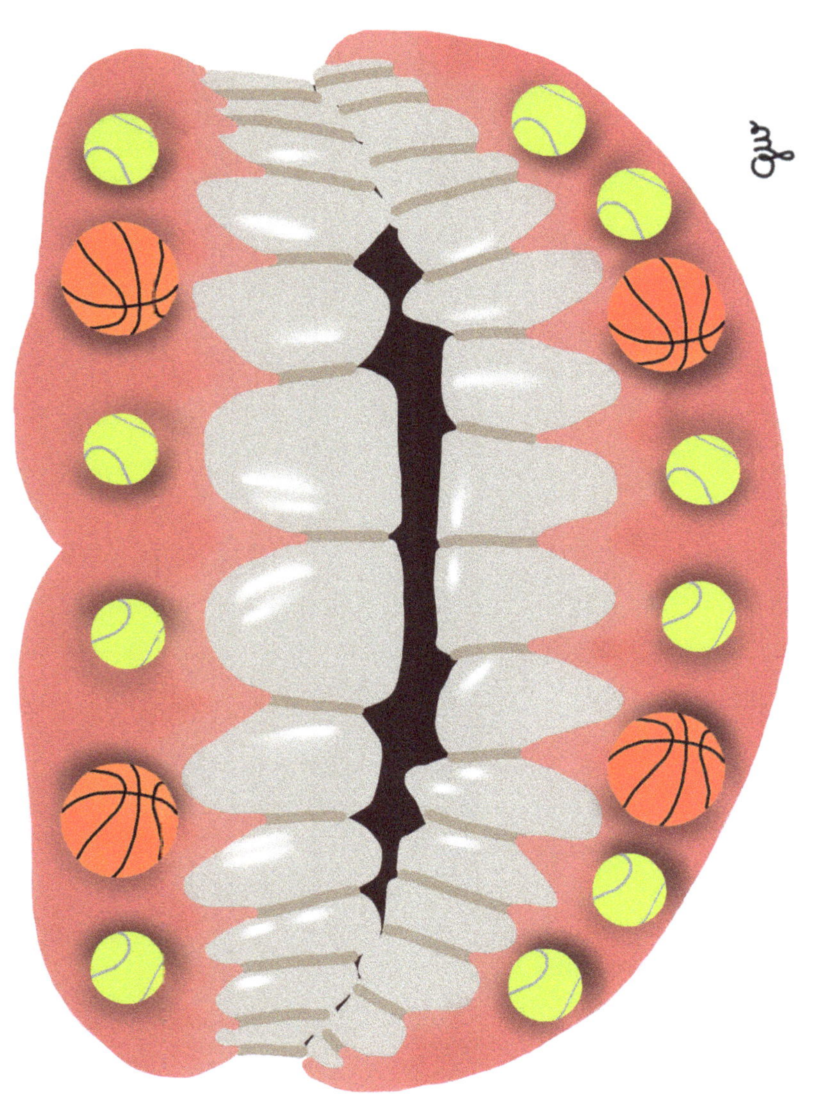

Gum Balls

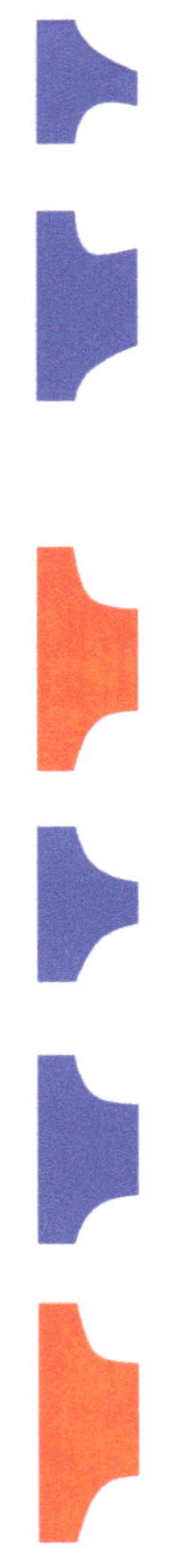

Fourth of July

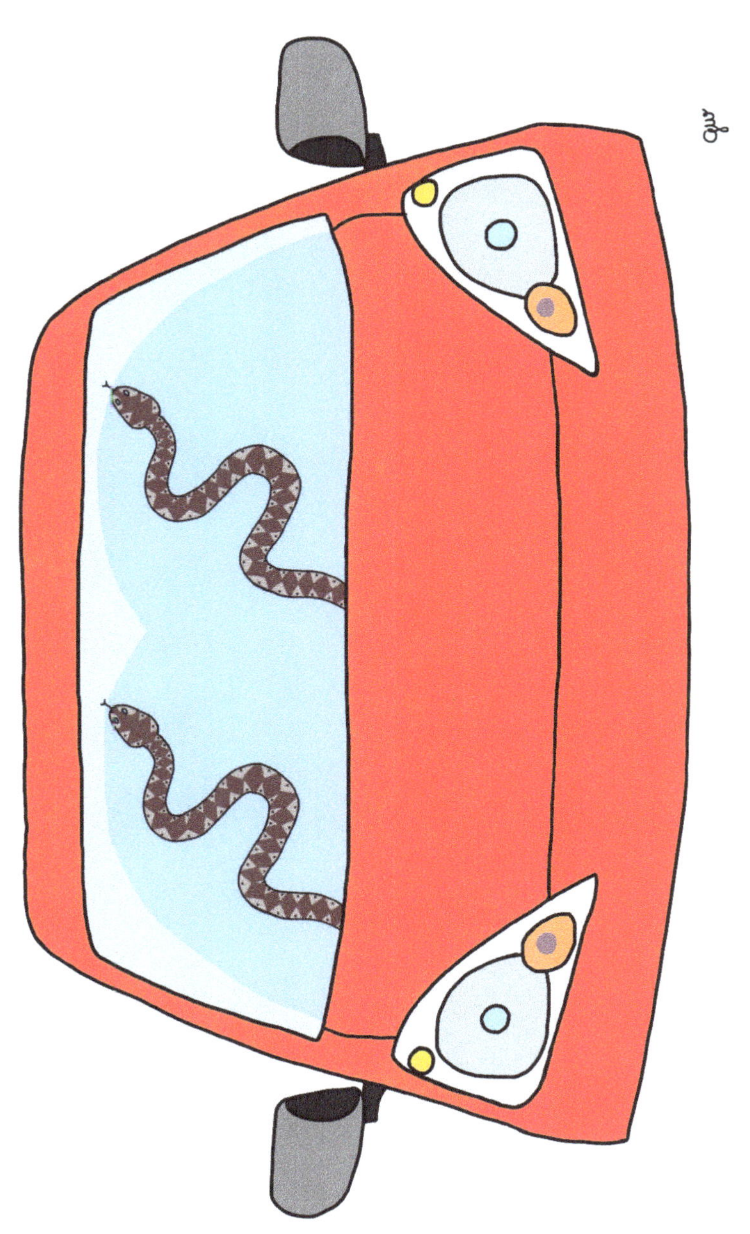

Windshield Vipers

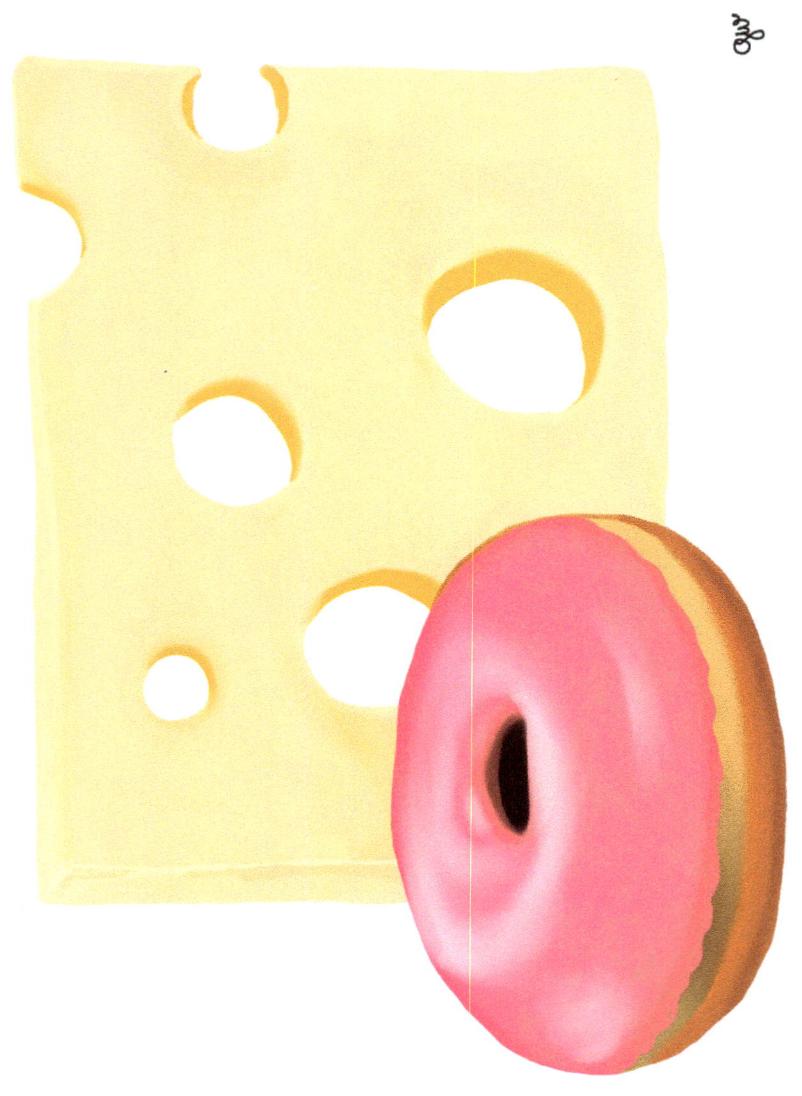

Hole Food

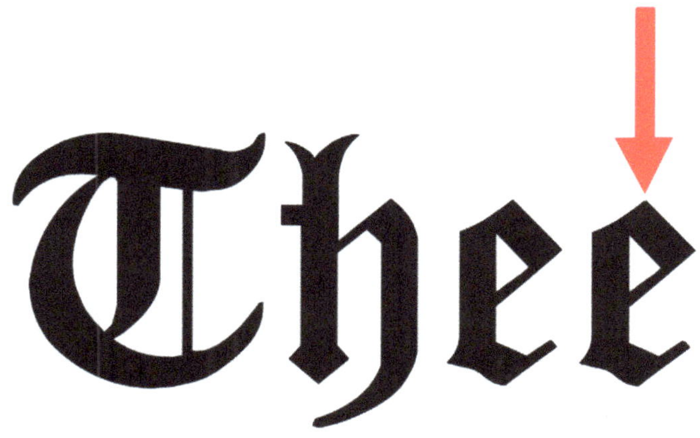

Thee End